GREATNESS IS UPON YOU !

Success Journal

HOW TO SEIZE AND SUSTAIN GREATNESS

ERIC THOMAS

SPIRIT REIGN PUBLISHING · A DIVISION OF SPIRIT REIGN COMMUNICATIONS

Author: Eric Thomas
Cover design: David Anderson
Page design & layout: Marie-Judith Jean-Louis
Illustrations : Marie-Judith Jean-Louis
http://mariejudith.com

Editor: Eric Thomas & Associates, LLC

Printed in the United States of America.

ISBN: 978-1-940002-40-8

TABLE OF CONTENTS

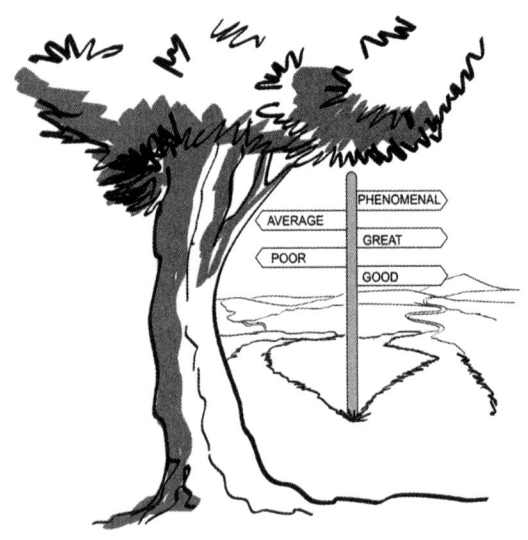

GETTING STARTED

What does it mean to be Great? By definition,

1.   of an extent, amount, or intensity considerably above the normal or average

2.   of ability, quality, or eminence considerably above normal or average

I say to people all the time that I am allergic to average but few people ever ask me what I mean by it. I have an aversion to average because average had the potential to be great but decided not to pursue it. Average is content with where he is. Average is doesn't make plans for his future. Average habitually sets goals with little to no intentions of seeing them through. Average sees failures as a burden and uses them to justify why he never got ahead in his career, why he never finished that book he wanted to write, why he never recorded that song he wrote, why he never saw his investment through, why he can't get along with his coworkers and family, why his relationships are short and unsalvageable, and why, for him, life is something that happens to you and not for you.

But in every situation, in every trial, in every outcome, Great is always above average, so if I had to choose between being great and being average - the choice is a no brainer. And the best news that I can give you is that no matter where you are in your life in this present moment, each of you have a quality inside of you that can enable you to achieve and sustain greatness in your careers, in school, in your relationships, and in every other area of your life. the secret is that there are no secrets, you simply have to be willing to sacrifice time and energy from some of the things that are hindering you from greatness and invest them into understanding these principles that will help you to re-evaluate and re-shape your life. greatness is upon you... act like it.

In GIUY, I outline 24 principles that I believe are instrumental in achieving Greatness. What does the word Great mean to you?

_____

_____

_____

_____

_____

_____

_____

How does your definition compare to what it means to be Average?

_____

_____

_____

_____

I think that there are so many examples of truly great figures today and throughout history:

Mother Teresa	Michael Jordan	Bill Gates
Ghandhi	Jesus Christ	Jackee Robinson
The Beatles	Mozart	Martin Luther King, Jr.
Bob Hope		

Who would you add to the chart above? Why?

_____

_____

_____

_____

How does your life, values, and principles compare to those listed?

_____

_____

_____

_____

_____

Now, answer the following:

When I look in the mirror, I can honestly say that **my life's choices** reflect my potential for greatness:
- ☐ 100% of the Time
- ☐ 80% of the time
- ☐ 50% of the time
- ☐ 30% of the time
- ☐ 29% or less of the time

When I look in the mirror, I can honestly say that **the friends that I've chosen** reflect my potential for greatness:
- ☐ 100% of the time
- ☐ 80% of the time
- ☐ 50% of the time
- ☐ 30% of the time
- ☐ 29% or less of the time

When I look in the mirror, I can honestly say that **the amount of time that I put into my goals** reflect my potential for greatness:
- ☐ 100% of the time
- ☐ 80% of the time
- ☐ 50% of the time
- ☐ 30% of the time
- ☐ 29% or less of the time

When I look in the mirror, I can honestly say that **the amount of time that I spend giving back to others** reflect my potential for greatness:
- ☐ 100% of the time
- ☐ 80% of the time
- ☐ 50% of the time
- ☐ 30% of the time
- ☐ 29% or less of the time

When I look in the mirror, i can honestly say that **my bank account** reflect my potential for greatness:
- ☐ 100% of the time
- ☐ 80% of the time
- ☐ 50% of the time
- ☐ 30% of the time
- ☐ 29% or less of the time

When I look in the mirror, i can honestly say that **my position at work** reflect my potential for greatness:
- ☐ 100% of the time
- ☐ 80% of the time
- ☐ 50% of the time
- ☐ 30% of the time
- ☐ 29% or less of the time

Now answer:

I am exactly where i want to be **financially** at this point in my life.
- ☐ Completely true
- ☐ Mostly true
- ☐ Somewhat true
- ☐ Not really true
- ☐ Not at all true

I am exactly where i want to be **physically** at this point in my life.
- ☐ Completely true
- ☐ Mostly true
- ☐ Somewhat true
- ☐ Not really true
- ☐ Not at all true

I am exactly where i want to be **professionally** at this point in my life.
- ☐ Completely true
- ☐ Mostly true
- ☐ Somewhat true
- ☐ Not really true
- ☐ Not at all true

I am exactly where i want to be in my **relationships** at this point in my life.
- ☐ Completely true
- ☐ Mostly true
- ☐ Somewhat true
- ☐ Not really true
- ☐ Not at all true

GREATNESS IS UPON YOU GREATNESS PRINCIPLE CHECK-LIST

Make each principle a goal and mark them off as you master them.

Date Mastered	Principles
☐	**Greatness Principle #1** Greatness is understanding that the bigger fear should not be in the realization of self but in its denial.
☐	**Greatness Principle #2** Greatness is being courageous enough to not let what matters most be put at the mercy of what matters least.
☐	**Greatness Principle #3** Greatness is being courageous enough to acknowledge your role in all that is wrong in your life and disciplined enough to not let it keep you from moving forward.
☐	**Greatness Principle #4** Greatness is impossible to obtain or sustain in the comfort of pessimism.
☐	**Greatness Principle #5** Greatness is acquiring a sense of what is necessary to prepare you for the life you were meant to live.
☐	**Greatness Principle #6** Greatness is exhausting every possibility from each opportunity.
☐	**Greatness Principle #7** Greatness is realizing that the dividing line between you and your competition is how prepared you came to fight.
☐	**Greatness Principle #8** Greatness is not taking for granted the lasting impact that giving to others can have on not just your life, but the lives of those you invested in.
☐	**Greatness Principle #9** Greatness is demonstrating humility in all aspects of life. If you can't reach back, you will never move forward.
☐	**Greatness Principle #10** Greatness is understanding the importance of service and selfless acts as being necessary for the betterment of all mankind.
☐	**Greatness Principle #11** Greatness is moving outside of your comfort zone, because out of your comfort zone is where the miracles happen. If it doesn't challenge you, it won't change you.
☐	**Greatness Principle #12** Greatness is deciding to take action, not just for your life, but for the lives of those who depend on you.

Date Mastered	Principles
☐	**Greatness Principle #13** Greatness is valuing the rewards of a mutual relationship over selfish ambition.
☐	**Greatness Principle #14** Greatness is acknowledging that as talented and successful as you may be, there is someone else who can show you more.
☐	**Greatness Principle #15** Greatness is not just seeking the information but acting on the body of knowledge you already have.
☐	**Greatness Principle #16** Greatness is saying, "Yes, I am afraid of failing, but I'm more afraid of failing to try."
☐	**Greatness Principle #17** Greatness is resisting the temptation to throw in the towel even when everything in your environment says you should.
☐	**Greatness Principle #18** Greatness is remembering in the dark what God told you in the light.
☐	**Greatness Principle #19** Greatness is the end result of consistency backed by an unbreachable promise.
☐	**Greatness Principle #20** Greatness is refusing to allow yourself to get beat out of the opportunity to fully realize your potential.
☐	**Greatness Principle #21** Greatness is not just about making the best out of whatever life gives you, it's also about commitment to your vision at all costs.
☐	**Greatness Principle #22** Greatness is expanding your portfolio to create more opportunities to stretch yourself.
☐	**Greatness Principle #23** Greatness is having the fortitude to get up after being knocked down.
☐	**Greatness Principle #24** Greatness is upon you.

WEEK 01
REPUTATION VS. CHARACTER

GREATNESS PRINCIPLE #1

Greatness is understanding that the bigger fear should not be in the realization of self but in its denial.

Do you spend more time building and protecting your reputation or developing your character?

In GIUY, I talk about one of my earliest encounters with having to make a decision between character and reputation. Think of a time in your life when you had to make a similar decision. What was the outcome?

DAY ONE: LEARN IT

REPUTATION
can be shifted

CHARACTER
your most valuable asset

Reputations can be shifted, people can see you as one thing one day and something completely different the next depending on the circumstances. Becoming Great requires an understanding that character is paramount to your success, because, unlike reputation, character is consistent.

Are you able to distinguish between who you are and what people think about you? How do you know?

_____

_____

_____

_____

_____

If reputations are like shadows, a mere facade of what truly exits, then why do we spend so much time trying to develop them?

_____

_____

_____

_____

Do you spend more time building your reputation or developing your character?

_____

_____

_____

_____

What are you **MOST** influenced by?

☐ Family

☐ Your Past

☐ Friends

☐ Money

☐ Power

☐ Your Environment

How does the item you checked influence your decisions on a daily basis?

_____

_____

_____

_____

DAY TWO: ACCEPT IT

Have you accepted the fact that your success is not about what people say about you but more about who you are?

CHARACTERISTICS OF REPUTATION AND CHARACTER	
Reputation	**Character**
Temporary *Rust* *Weak Foundation*	*Eternal* *Rust Proof* *Solid Foundation*

Now, considering the descriptions in the chart above for both reputation and character, in the table below, identify what people commonly say about you (your reputation) and then identify your principles/who you are at your core (your character). What are the consistencies or inconsistencies between the two?

Reputation	Character

DAY THREE: EMBRACE IT

Character flaws don't have to be permanent. Ask yourself:

Am I consistently honest with myself and others about who I am?	☐ Yes ☐ No	Why?
Am I loyal to my principles and values?	☐ Yes ☐ No	Why?
Do I habitually invest in the interests of others?	☐ Yes ☐ No	Why?
Do I take ownership for the mistakes that I make in life?	☐ Yes ☐ No	Why?

On Day Two, after listing those things that people often say about you, you should have listed your principles and core values - things that would describe your character. Today, describe those characteristics of yours that would be considered a flaw in character.

_____

_____

_____

_____

_____

DAY FOUR: CHANGE IT

HOW WILL YOU WORK TO IMPROVE IN EACH AREA ?

create a game plan

Trust is the catalyst for success. Learn to establish trust by strengthening your core:

1. Make choices that coincide with who you want to be.
2. Always apply the Golden Rule: Treat others the way you want to be treated.
3. Embrace every opportunity to show people that you care.
4. Take responsibility for your actions.
5. No one trusts a cheat - play fair and stay fair.

Answer the following:
People know what they can expect from me 100% of the time

☐ Completely True   ☐ Mostly True   ☐ Somewhat True   ☐ Not Quite True   ☐ Never

Choose three of the areas you identified from Day Three, and create a game plan detailing how you will work to improve in each of the areas that you noted as character flaws using the core-strengthening activities on the previous page.

Area 1 : _____

_____

_____

_____

_____

_____

Area 2 : _____

_____

_____

_____

_____

_____

Area 3 : _____

_____

_____

_____

_____

DAY FIVE: LIVE IT

Are you ready to live a life that focuses on building your character more than your reputation? Write out your 7-day plan to live a life that focuses more on your character than your reputation.
Don't forget to use the core-strengthening activities listed in Day Four.

Sunday _____

_____

_____

Monday _____

_____

_____

Tuesday _____

_____

_____

Wednesday _____

_____

_____

_____

Thursday _____

_____

_____

Friday _____

_____

_____

Saturday _____

_____

_____

GREATNESS IS...

Martin Luther King Jr. said it best when he said, "The ultimate measure of a man is not where he stands in moments of comfort and conveniences, but where he stands at times of challenge and controversy." Where do you stand in your darkest hours? Where do you stand when the very people you thought were in your corner are suddenly giving you up to the wolves? Where will you stand when you're faced with the decision between upholding your standard or buying in to the status quo?

You will never know the magnitude of your potential if external circumstances (your past, finances, people, your environment, etc.) have the ability to influence who you become. You will never realize success if your integrity is dispensable. You will never achieve Greatness if the measure of your worth is scaled by how often others praise or applaud you. Who are you when the stage clears and there is no one left in the audience?

What causes us to value reputation over character? Fear. If you never have to face who you are at your core, you never have to put in the work to develop it. We don't want to see the dark and the ugly, because then we have to make a decision to leave it there or change it.

Greatness is understanding that the bigger fear should not be in the realization of self but in its denial.

Spend time today reflecting on your actions this week.

Did you meet the challenge? If not, why?

_____

_____

_____

_____

GREATNESS IS UPON YOU

GREATNESS IS UPON YOU

CERTIFICATE OF COMPLETION

This is to certify that

_____

has successfully completed this week's challenge.

Eric Thomas and Associates, LLC

_____

signature

_____

date

Week 02
GETTING CAUGHT VS. CONFESSION
GREATNESS PRINCIPLE #2:
Greatness is being courageous enough to not let what matters most be put at the mercy of what matters least.

If you had to make a choice between confessing the truth from the beginning or waiting it out until you got caught, which would you choose?

In the previous chapter, I told you about the fickle nature of reputation and why it's so important to focus on developing your core. This week, we're going to take a closer look at what happens when we place a higher value on maintaining our reputation at the expense of our character.

Begin by answering the following questions. In any given situation, if confessing the truth meant:

Losing my job, I would still tell the truth.	☐ True	☐ False
Losing my friends, I would still tell the truth.	☐ True	☐ False
Losing my financial status, I would still tell the truth.	☐ True	☐ False
Losing my credibility, I would still tell the truth	☐ True	☐ False

If it wasn't easy to answer on paper, it definitely wouldn't be easy in real life. The fact is, its rarely ever this black and white, and yet, it should be. What is the one event or situation that made or could make the above statements false?

_____

_____

_____

_____

_____

_____

_____

_____

_____

DAY ONE: LEARN IT

Several times in the media, we've seen leaders of universities and churches exposed for criminal or fraudulent activities that many others were aware of but never disclosed the truth about because they were concerned about what the exposure would do for their reputations. When maintaing your reputation fails you, what do you have left standing in the balance?

_____

_____

_____

_____

_____

REMEMBER:

- Reputations are like shadows - they are images that can easily be manipulated by external sources (i.e., people, gossip, unexpected circumstances, etc.).

- Character is who you really are - it can be developed or underdeveloped, but only you can control it.

- Reputations can be good or bad but are ultimately unstable. When more value is placed in maintaining or building your reputation than the building of your character, you risk compromising your integrity.

Think through these principles throughout the day.

_____

_____

_____

_____

DAY TWO: ACCEPT IT

IDENTIFY at least one image that you have worked desperately to maintain and the things that you've done to keep that reputation.

Be honest with yourself and record your answers below:

_____

_____

_____

_____

_____

_____

DAY THREE: EMBRACE IT

Identify a time when you valued your reputation more than your character. What domino effect did it create? Write out your domino effect below.

What are the benefits in maintaining your character instead?

_____

_____

_____

_____

_____

DAY FOUR: CHANGE IT

WHAT WILL YOU DO TODAY TO INTERCEPT THE DOMINO EFFECT

**CHANGE WHAT
COULD OTHERWISE
BE A CATASTROPHIC END**

The switch to focusing on character development requires honesty with yourself as well as others. This is the difference between confession and getting caught. What will you do today to intercept the domino effect?

_____

_____

_____

_____

_____

_____

_____

_____

_____

_____

DAY FIVE: LIVE IT

This is your opportunity to invest in your core. How will you build on your character? Create a 7-day plan to move from valuing your reputation more than your character.

Sunday _____

_____

_____

Monday _____

_____

_____

Tuesday _____

_____

_____

Wednesday _____

_____

_____

Thursday _____

_____

_____

Friday _____

_____

_____

Saturday _____

_____

_____

GREATNESS IS...

There's an old story about the son of a King who was instructed to go to war with their country's biggest enemy. This enemy had such hatred for the people of their land that the father knew that leaving anyone alive would ultimately lead to the destruction of their own people. So the father told his son to completely destroy the entire enemy army and all of their spoils - he was to take no prisoners.

The son desired more than anything to be seen as powerful and unyielding, and he had developed a reputation among his people as one to be feared. In war, the son battled courageously, but instead of instructing his men according to the directions of his father, he told them to leave the enemy's king alive. He knew that doing so would not only send a message to everyone in the kingdom about the extent of his prowess, but the enemy king himself would live to tell the story of how the son had defeated him and was gracious enough to leave him alive.

When word of the son's disobedience made it back to the King, he was sorely disappointed. As it was written, an infraction such as this was punishable by death. To sacrifice the lives and well being of his own people to be seen as powerful was deplorable. But instead of immediate death, the King ripped the son of all of his power and title. Devastated, the son went through a major psychosis, lost everything he ever loved, and eventually died in war. But worst of all, the long-term effect of the son's disobedience would soon be felt. The enemy king lived and, years later, the enemy King's offspring came back and destroyed all of the Monarch's people.

Working to maintain your reputation is possibly the most damaging thing you could do to your success. Character sustains what fictitious images won't. In the story, the King's son was willing to put his whole country at risk to have people think that he was powerful and, in the end, his shortsightedness cost him everything. What are you putting in the line of fire to protect what people think of you? Who are you willing to hurt? What are you willing to go through?

It's easy to say you don't care what people say or think about you, but do your actions reflect that?

Greatness is being courageous enough to not let what matters most be put at the mercy of what matters least.

Spend time today reflecting on your actions this week.

Did you meet the challenge? If not, why?

_____

_____

_____

_____

_____

GIUY RE-UP

Weeks 1 and 2 specifically addressed character and reputation.
Remember:

AVERAGE PEOPLE	GREATNESS...
Value what other people think about them more than developing their core.	Requires a commitment to strengthening and developing your core.
Are inconsistent with representing who they are.	Requires an alignment between your core beliefs and your actions.
Can't be trusted because they are inconsistent (see above).	Requires an ability to be trusted by people in your environment.
Try to cover up flaws to make themselves look better.	Requires exposure of the truth with the intent to become better.
Go out of their way to protect or maintain their image.	Requires commitment to integrity.

Assess how well you've demonstrated your potential in this area on the scales below:

Before reading:

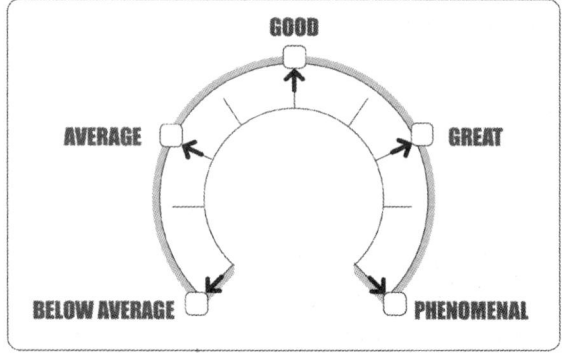

After Reading:

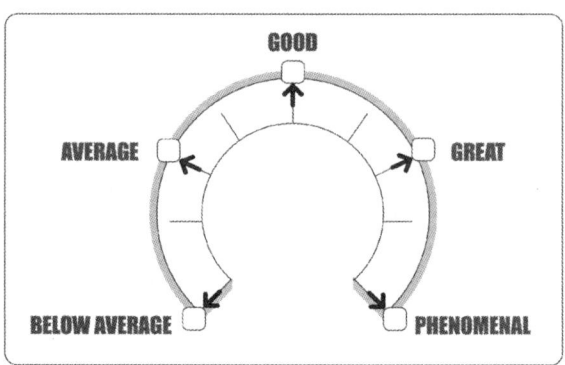

_____

_____

_____

_____

_____

_____

_____

_____

GREATNESS IS UPON YOU

CERTIFICATE OF COMPLETION

This is to certify that

_____

has successfully completed this week's challenge.

Eric Thomas and Associates, LLC

_____
signature

_____
date

Week 03
VICTIM VS. VICTOR
GREATNESS PRINCIPLE #3:

Greatness is being courageous enough to acknowledge your role in all that is wrong in your life and disciplined enough to not let it keep you from moving forward.

Do you view the world in terms of what you've been slighted or in terms of what you can get out of it?

If you see or feel anything within yourself that remotely looks like a Victim's Mentality, run from it like it's the Bubonic Plague! Don't allow yourself to become a victim of this illness. I am passionate about this, because I know about this disease what the people of the 14th Century knew about the Bubonic Plague - if you stay in the environment where the disease has manifested itself - then it's inevitable that you will die.

Most people have felt at least once in their life, that things would be different for them if their circumstances were different. If this applies to you, write about that event or situation below. Get it out of your system now, because after today, your goal should be to never look at that event or situation the same.

_____

_____

_____

_____

_____

_____

_____

_____

_____

_____

_____

_____

DAY ONE: LEARN IT

CHALLENGES AND DISAPPOINTMENTS

What role did/do you play in them?

What was your thought process throughout this difficult time?

What decisions did you ultimately make?

FIRED

Consider the challenges and disappointments you presently face in your life.

_____

_____

_____

_____

What role did/do you play in them?

_____

_____

_____

_____

What was your thought process throughout this difficult time?

_____

_____

_____

_____

_____

What decisions did you ultimately make? How did these decisions affect the outcome?

_____

_____

_____

_____

What could you have done differently to achieve a more positive result?

_____

_____

_____

_____

THOUGHTS ⟩ DECISIONS ⟩ ACTIONS ⟩ RESULTS

VICTOR
TAKING
OWNERSHIP

VS

VICTIM
PLAYING THE
BLAME GAME

Our thoughts, decisions, and actions play a significant role in the results we get out of life.

When I changed the way I thought about the circumstances surrounding my speaking career to something more positive, it enabled me to make better decisions and eventually led to more favorable results.

Make a list of the most devastating challenges that have had an impact on your personal or professional life (i.e., fired from a job/death of a loved one).

_____

_____

_____

_____

Place each major challenge under one of the areas below.

_____

challenges that are out of your control	challenges that you can manipulate
i.e. I was a first generation college student.	*I didn't utilize my resources.* *I didn't put forth my best effort in college.* *I didn't ask for help when I needed it.*

How did the challenges you can manipulate help you to develop or hinder you personally or professionally?

_____

_____

_____

_____

DAY TWO: ACCEPT IT

One major disappointment in my life was when _____

_____

_____

_____

_____

_____

During this time, I was thinking _____

_____

_____

_____

_____

_____

_____

My actions involved me _____

_____

_____

_____

_____

_____

_____

As a result, I _____

_____

_____

_____

_____

_____

_____

_____

One Step Further: If you are a visual learner, you can do the same activity above by placing your answers in a diagram similar to the one below:

THOUGHTS	DECISIONS	ACTIONS	RESULTS
"If he doesn't give me the promotion, I'll quit." "I'm tired of being overworked and underappreciated." "That's it, I'm done."	Decide to stop giving your best effort. Decided to disconnect and become aloof and distant.	Stop coming to work on time. Start turning in your assignments late.	Get fired or laid off or You miss the next promotion opportunity

DAY THREE: EMBRACE IT

Complete the statement below:

I would have been able to do _____

_____

if _____

_____ *had done his/her part or*

This would not have happened if it weren't for _____

_____

LOOK AT YOURSELF IN THE MIRROR
ADMIT YOUR ROLE IN YOUR DISAPPOINTMENT

Today, you are going to practice taking ownership for the role you played in your tragedy.

Look at yourself in the mirror (i.e., bathroom mirror, handheld mirror, hallway mirror, etc.) and verbally admit to yourself your role in the disappointment you wrote about yesterday. Explain to yourself how your behavior led to the end results.

Example: "I was fired from my job, because I got upset about not getting the promotion I wanted; I stopped giving my best effort at work and started coming in late."

_____

_____

_____

_____

DAY FOUR: CHANGE IT
GET UNSOLVED FEELINGS OUT OF YOUR SYSTEM

Today, write a letter to the other player(s) involved in the disappointment that you have been focusing on this week (i.e., your boss, your teacher/professor, an old friend, spouse, etc.). Identify both of your roles in the disappointment and be honest about how the situation made you feel. Don't be afraid to write this letter 3, 4, or even 5 times if necessary. I DO NOT recommend that you burn the letters, but ball each one up and throw them away as you finish. Remember, the goal is not to deliver this letter but to get unresolved feelings out of your system. Sometimes change simply involves handling things in a way you never would have considered before. This assignment is meant to be a therapeutic means for you to get some things out of your system that may be holding you back from becoming a Victor. You can create a draft of your letter below.

_____

_____

_____

_____

_____

_____

DAY FIVE: TEACH IT

Write a 7-day plan to shift from victim to victor.
Consider things in your life that you do habitually that have contributed to upsets on a consistent basis. Before you begin your journey, go back to the same mirror you stood in front of earlier this week, and vow to make the necessary changes to your character.

Sunday _____

_____

_____

Monday _____

_____

_____

Tuesday _____

_____

_____

Wednesday _____

_____

_____

Thursday _____

_____

_____

Friday _____

_____

_____

Saturday _____

_____

_____

GREATNESS IS...

Albert Einstein said that "man must cease attributing his problems to his environment, and learn again to exercise his will – his personal responsibility."

What if Einstein, in the midst of being underestimated by his teachers, being misunderstood at home and in school, and having a father who had multiple failed businesses, saw himself as a mere victim in a world of a series of unfortunate life-altering events? What if he waited for his professors to affirm his intellect? What if he made a commitment to resentment instead of responsibility? What if he stifled his gifts and talents so that he could instead voice his discontentment with the people in his environment? What if Einstein chose to blame his parents' failures for his own failures and became content with mediocrity at the expense of Greatness?

The answer is simple: we would be acknowledging someone else for revolutionizing the way we see science.

We are all one complaint or rationalization away from someone else doing what you were meant to do. Because while you're wasting time complaining and placing blame on other people and circumstances, someone else is exercising his or her will and taking responsibility for his or her actions so that he or she can claim Victory out of life and not be victimized by a defeatist mentality.

Greatness is being courageous enough to acknowledge your role in all that is wrong in your life and disciplined enough to not let it keep you from moving forward.

Spend time today reflecting on your actions this week.

Did you meet the challenge? If not, why?

_____

_____

_____

_____

_____

_____

_____

_____

_____

_____

GREATNESS IS UPON YOU

CERTIFICATE OF COMPLETION

This is to certify that

_____

has successfully completed this week's challenge.

Eric Thomas and Associates, LLC

_____
signature

_____
date

WEEK 04
NEGATIVE THINKING VS. POSITIVE THINKING
GREATNESS PRINCIPLE #4:
Greatness is impossible to obtain or sustain in the comfort of pessimism.

From where you stand, is the glass half full or not even worth the effort?

In the previous chapter, we discussed that the way you think has a significant impact on the results that you get out of life. In this chapter, we take a closer look at the effects of negative thinking and how you can systematically deprogram from habitual negative thinking to positive thinking.

At times, my thoughts have made me feel sad, unhappy, or depressed	☐ True ☐ False	*If true, how did you behave or respond in that moment?*
At times, my thoughts have made me feel angry, rejected, or unwanted.	☐ True ☐ False	*If true, how did you behave or respond in that moment?*
At times, my thoughts have caused me to remember painful events from my past	☐ True ☐ False	*If true, how did you behave or respond in that moment?*
At times, my thoughts have made me feel motivated, inspired, or uplifted.	☐ True ☐ False	*If true, how did you behave or respond in that moment?*
At times, my thoughts have moved me to do something nice for someone.	☐ True ☐ False	*If true, how did you behave or respond in that moment?*
At times, my thoughts have caused me to have memories of happy moments in my life.	☐ True ☐ False	*If true, how did you behave or respond in that moment?*

DAY ONE: LEARN IT

What mental adjustments do you need to make to better position yourself in your career, academic life, social life, or family life?

_____

_____

_____

_____

_____

_____

Are you able to see how your thoughts affect your behavior?

_____

_____

_____

_____

_____

_____

_____

_____

DAY TWO: ACCEPT IT

Accepting that your thoughts influence your actions may be difficult, but I challenge you to look deeply at some areas in your life that aren't going well to see if you can find some commonalities in the type of thinking that you're doing and the outcome. Follow the steps below to complete the diagram for an area in your life that you are currently experiencing a CHALLENGE in when it comes to the way you think:

IDENTIFY your CHALLENGE area.

_____

Describe the thoughts that you commonly have in that area.

_____

_____

_____

_____

_____

Describe the things that you commonly **say** concerning that area in your life. (This can be things that you say to other people or things that you say to yourself.)

_____

_____

_____

_____

_____

Describe your **behavior** in that area (use action words).

_____

_____

_____

_____

_____

DAY THREE: EMBRACE IT

Even if you are completely justified, the wrong impression can be extensively damaging to your success. Look at the same situation you journaled about on Day Two and think through positive ways to think, speak, and ultimately behave in that situation.

Thinking - How can you think differently to reposition yourself for success in your CHALLENGE area from yesterday?

_____

_____

_____

_____

_____

Speaking - How can you speak differently to reposition yourself for success in your CHALLENGE area from yesterday?

_____

_____

_____

_____

_____

Behaving - What can you physically do differently to reposition yourself for success in your CHALLENGE area from yesterday?

_____

_____

_____

_____

_____

Be sure to think through how your thoughts and language should change in order to see a successful change in your behavior.

DAY FOUR: CHANGE IT

Now that you've thought of ways to change your thinking, speaking, and behavior (Day Two), address what general changes in your speech and actions/behaviors you and the people around you can expect to see as a result of your decision to engage in more positive thoughts.

In the chart below, list the different changes in your speech that you plan to make and the actions you can commit to changing on the regular.

SPEAKING	what actions will i see as a result of the changes ?
i.e., I will speak more positively about my student's behavior.	_I won't be as frustrated with my student and my positive attitude will have a lasting impact on my student as well as my colleagues._

Write about a time when your thoughts pushed you to do something positive that you didn't think you could do. Did it encourage you? Encourage 2-3 other people with your story to inspire them to change their course as well.

_____

_____

_____

_____

_____

_____

DAY FIVE: LIVE IT

Create a 7-day plan for how you will actively work to change the way that you think. Be sure to include extra meditation and reflection time in your plan so that you can learn what negative thoughts trigger your negative behaviors.

Sunday _____

_____

_____

Monday _____

_____

_____

Tuesday _____

_____

_____

Wednesday _____

_____

_____

Thursday _____

_____

_____

Friday _____

_____

_____

Saturday _____

_____

_____

GREATNESS IS...

"Either make the tree sound (healthy and good), and its fruit sound (healthy and good), or make the tree rotten (diseased and bad), and its fruit rotten (diseased and bad); for the tree is known and recognized and judged by its fruit ." [Matthew 12:33 Amplified Bible]

The reason we fall prey to negative thinking is because it's easy.

When the children are getting on your nerves; when your boss doesn't notice your hard work; when you didn't get accepted into the school or program you dreamed of getting into; when your employees don't seem to get the vision of the company and productivity is slow; when the bills are piling up; when you're still looking in the face of unemployment; when the doctors have given you bad news; when you're fed up, tired, and lonely the most comfortable place in the world is Pessimism. It quenches the thirst of disappointment.

Positive thoughts in the midst of struggles are challenging because it forces you to consider and then believe that which is invisible in the moment of your trial. Either make the tree sound and let it Bear good fruit or make it rotten and let it Bear bad fruit. Life isn't easy so the way that you process it isn't going to be either.

Greatness is impossible to obtain or sustain in the comfort of pessimism.

Spend time today reflecting on your actions this week.

Did you meet the challenge? If not, why?

_____

_____

_____

_____

_____

_____

GREATNESS IS UPON YOU

CERTIFICATE OF COMPLETION

This is to certify that

_____

has successfully completed this week's challenge.

Eric Thomas and Associates, LLC

_____
signature

_____
date

WEEK 05
GRASSHOPPER VS. ANT
GREATNESS PRINCIPLE #5:
Greatness is acquiring a sense of what is necessary to prepare you for the life you were meant to live.

Are you missing out on opportunities or taking advantage of what life brings you?

I've learned that there's no such thing as procrastination (at least not in the way that most people use the word), it's more an issue of priority. All of the things I had going on at the time were legitimate, but my priorities were misaligned. I didn't miss out on an opportunity to take advantage of a million-dollar investment because I was lazy, disinterested, or unmotivated; it was because, as crazy as it sounds, the investment wasn't a number one priority for me.

Which category do you fit into?

☐	I know exactly what level of priority to give EVERY agenda in my life and I follow through EVERY time.
☐	I somewhat know what level of priority to give most agendas in my life and I try to follow through but sometimes fail.
☐	I never know what level of priority to give things that come up in my life so I just go with the flow.

How effective has your system proven to be? Hint: There's always room for improvement.

_____

_____

_____

_____

_____

_____

_____

_____

_____

DAY ONE: LEARN IT

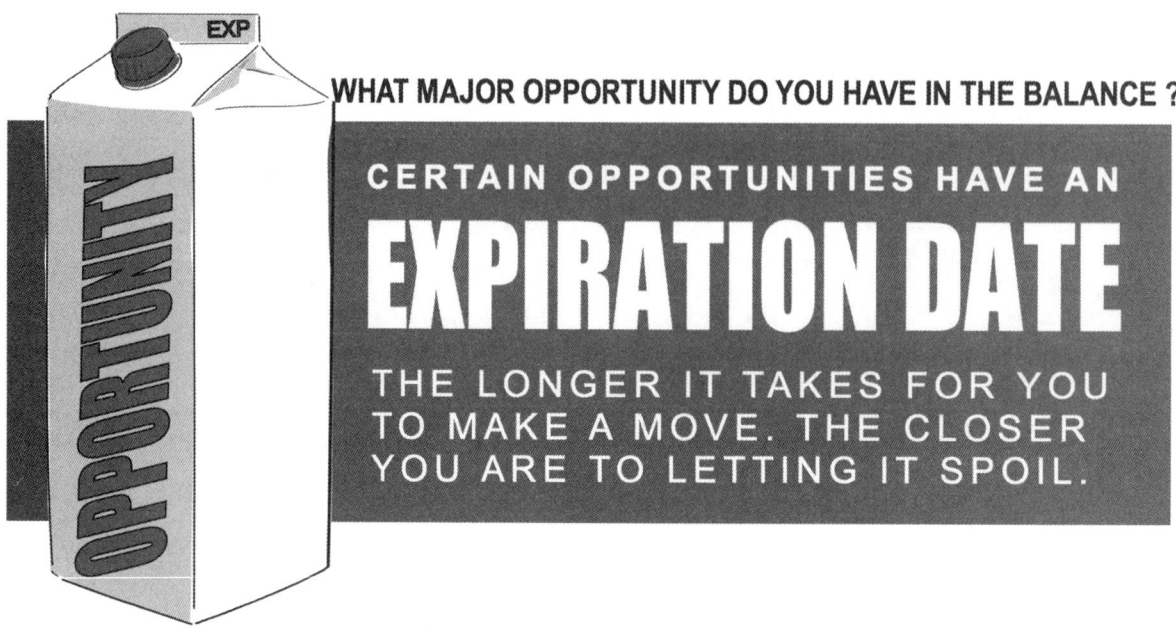

WHAT MAJOR OPPORTUNITY DO YOU HAVE IN THE BALANCE ?

CERTAIN OPPORTUNITIES HAVE AN

EXPIRATION DATE

THE LONGER IT TAKES FOR YOU TO MAKE A MOVE. THE CLOSER YOU ARE TO LETTING IT SPOIL.

What major opportunities do you have sitting in the balance?

_____

_____

_____

_____

_____

Why haven't you taken advantage of them?

_____

_____

_____

_____

_____

_____

DAY TWO: ACCEPT IT

In the table below, list the "Things that are Important to You" in column A and the "Things that are Expected of You, but aren't Important to You" in column B.

A important to you	B expected of you

On the balance beam on the next page, list those things from columns A and B above that you spend most of your time doing on the left. Then list those things that you don't spend as much time doing from columns A and B on the right side of the balance beam. Are you spending more time doing things that are important to you or things that are not important to you?

DAY THREE: EMBRACE IT

EMERGENCY
VERY
IMPORTANT
IMPORTANT
NOT
IMPORTANT

What do you have going on in your life? Today, make a list of all your goals or make a list of all your responsibilities, and prioritize them according to the scale above.

Goals, Responsibilities, and Priorities

_____

_____

_____

_____

_____

_____

_____

_____

_____

_____

_____

_____

_____

_____

_____

_____

_____

_____

_____

_____

_____

DAY FOUR: CHANGE IT

Begin with today in mind. Yesterday, you prioritized all of your goals and /or responsibilities. Today, prioritize all of your activities for today in order of **Emergency** to **Not Important** and complete activities from your list in the order of importance.

EMERGENCY	☐
	☐
	☐
	☐
	☐
VERY IMPORTANT	☐
	☐
	☐
	☐
	☐
IMPORTANT	☐
	☐
	☐
	☐
	☐
NOT IMPORTANT	☐
	☐
	☐
	☐
	☐

What items are on your plate? Rank them from most important (1) to not important (6). Also, IDENTIFY the people that also depend on those tasks to be done.*

* Each arm should represent a different item on your plate.

The key is not to prioritize what's on your schedule, but to schedule your priorities.
- *Stephen Covey*

Schedule your priorities.

Use the schedule below to **CREATE** a day where you schedule your priorities, instead of prioritizing whats on your schedule.

5AM _____

_____

6AM _____

_____

7AM _____

_____

8AM _____

_____

9AM _____

_____

10AM _____

_____

11AM _____

_____

12PM_____

_____

1PM _____

_____

2PM _____

_____

3PM _____

_____

4PM _____

_____

5PM _____

_____

6PM _____

_____

7PM _____

_____

8PM _____

_____

DAY FIVE: LIVE IT

Create a 7-day plan to take advantage of all of your opportunities.

Sunday _____

_____

_____

Monday _____

_____

_____

Tuesday _____

_____

_____

Wednesday _____

_____

_____

Thursday _____

_____

_____

Friday _____

_____

_____

Saturday _____

_____

_____

GREATNESS IS...

There is a fable that I used to hear when I was a kid about the grasshopper and the ant. In the story, the grasshopper sees a group of ants carrying kernels of corn and wants to know what they're getting ready to do with them. When one ant, too busy to talk, tells him that they're taking the kernels to their hill to store food for the winter, the grasshopper wanted to sing and play music instead. By the end of the fable, the winter weather comes, and the grasshopper is left hungry and unprepared.

My teacher would tell us this story to illustrate the importance of hard work and the evils of procrastination. To me, the issue for the grasshopper was never that he didn't want to prepare for the winter; it was that at the time when the opportunity was presented to him, there was something else that was more important to him, and he took for granted that the window to gather food would be available to him when he was ready to return to it. He made the mistake that we all are guilty of making at some point in our life - he underestimated the life span of the opportunity.

You will never be successful if you don't learn how to recognize those moments in your life that require you to make an immediate move.

Consider this: who were you supposed to be by now? CEO of your company? A college graduate? A lawyer? A leader in your community? Financially independent? How many life changing moments have you already let pass you by?

The grasshopper was bigger, stronger, and possibly faster, but he starved that winter. Why? Because he was ignorant to the value of what sacrificing something that he really wanted in that moment would bring to him in the future.

Because opportunities have a time frame, you can be stronger, smarter, and more passionate than the competition and still not make it to where you're supposed to be, because you never learned how to properly align your priorities.

Greatness is acquiring a sense of what is necessary to prepare you for the life you were meant to live.

Spend time today reflecting on your actions this week.

Did you meet the challenge? If not, why?

_____

If you could be more, see more, have more...what would it look like? How can you use the momentum you currently have to get it?

GREATNESS IS UPON YOU

CERTIFICATE OF COMPLETION

This is to certify that

_____

has successfully completed this week's challenge.

Eric Thomas and Associates, LLC

_____
signature

_____
date

WEEK 06
MINIMIZE VS. OPTIMIZE
GREATNESS PRINCIPLE #6:
Greatness is exhausting every possibility from each opportunity.

Are you squeezing everything you can get out of the opportunities you're taking advantage of or are you leaving behind residual opportunities?

Last week we discussed the importance of taking advantage of the opportunity of a lifetime in the lifetime of the opportunity, but what do you do once you've made your move? This chapter focuses on how to get the most out of the opportunities you want to take advantage of.

_____

_____

_____

_____

_____

_____

_____

_____

_____

_____

_____

_____

_____

_____

DAY ONE: LEARN IT

ARE YOU GETTING THE MOST OUT OF EVERY OPPORTUNITY YOU'RE INVESTESTING IN ?

The path from below average to becoming Great is going to require you to optimize every opportunity. Are you getting the most out of every opportunity you're investing in?

_____

_____

_____

_____

_____

_____

_____

_____

_____

DAY TWO: ACCEPT IT

3 COMMON OBSTACLES
that cause us to miss out on getting the most out of our opportunities

IGNORANCE
CONFIDENCE
INABILITY TO FORECAST

Acceptance is one of the most difficult parts of growth, but without it you'll never move beyond Average. Which of these reasons are getting in the way of you being able to get the most out of every opportunity?

Ignorance
☐ Yes ☐ Sometimes ☐ No

Confidence
☐ Yes ☐ Sometimes ☐ No

Procrastination
☐ Yes ☐ Sometimes ☐ No

Taking shortcuts are only beneficial when they effectively help you to reach your goal. Most times, they don't work. I've learned that it is far more beneficial in the long run to focus on the most effective way (not the quickest way) to meet your goals. Otherwise, you may miss out on opportunities. It's no different than when a teacher tells a student to work a math problem out instead of simply writing the answer. There are growth opportunities between the beginning and the end. Using the chart below identify goals that you've been working on and compare what the difference would be in taking a short cut versus optimizing the opportunity.

My Goals	Shortcut	Optimizing the Opportunity

DAY THREE: EMBRACE IT

Now that you know at least three different obstacles that get in the way of you being able to capitalize on every opportunity, address your reason for why you have been ignorant, lacked confidence, and/or unable to forecast for so long.

_____

_____

_____

_____

_____

DAY FOUR: CHANGE IT

What changes do you need to make to overcome the obstacles that you identified

MOVE BEYOND AVERAGE

What changes do you need to make to overcome the obstacles that you identified yesterday?

_____

_____

_____

_____

_____

_____

Share your ideas with a friend or mentor to gain a different perspective.

Which of the 5 techniques on the previous page will you use to optimize your opportunities? Give examples, so you are able to refer to the plan and goal you have set for yourself.

_____

_____

_____

_____

_____

DAY FIVE: LIVE IT

You can use this week to practice the changes that you listed yesterday. Create a 7-day plan to take advantage of all of your opportunities.

Sunday _____

_____

Monday _____

_____

Tuesday _____

_____

Wednesday _____

_____

Thursday _____

_____

_____

Friday _____

_____

_____

Saturday _____

_____

_____

GREATNESS IS...

Candy Crush Saga will probably go down in history as one of the most popular social games to ever be developed. Today, it averages over 40 million users a month and is played over 600 million times a day. I can't get on a plane or walk into a building without either hearing someone talk about it or seeing someone playing it on their cell phone. I think the word that best describes it is: addictive.

King is the casual-social games company that developed Candy Crush Saga; and what I love about King is that the company illustrates what happens when you optimize an opportunity. King started with only a handful of entrepreneurs and, ten years later, it has one of the highest grossing social games to ever exist. The company revolutionized the game industry by going one step further than its competition - King made it possible for people to play their game across multiple platforms and still keep their place. Meaning, if you start playing on Facebook you could pick up where you left off on your mobile device.

King could have been content with just having Candy Crush be like any other multi-platform game but the company optimized what users would be able to do with it and in turn guaranteed its success.

It's not enough to just take advantage of an opportunity. What happens after you take the job offer? What's the next step after writing your book or paying for studio time to record your single? How many new steps can be created from your first step?

Greatness is exhausting every possibility from each opportunity.

Spend time today reflecting on your actions this week.

Did you meet the challenge? If not, why?

_____

_____

_____

_____

_____

GREATNESS IS UPON YOU

CERTIFICATE OF COMPLETION

This is to certify that

_____

has successfully completed this week's challenge.

Eric Thomas and Associates, LLC

_____

signature

_____

date

WEEK 07
UNDER COMPETITION VS. COMPETITIVE EDGE
GREATNESS PRINCIPLE #7:
Greatness is realizing that the dividing line between you and your competition is how prepared you came to fight.

Do you step into the ring prepared for the fight or prepared for the win?

I loved the interview that Ali had before his fight with Foreman. Aside from it being hilarious, it illustrated one fundamental point that's necessary for achieving Greatness: to be Great, you must plan with a vision in mind.

What is the difference between preparing for the fight and preparing for the win?

_____

_____

_____

_____

_____

_____

_____

_____

_____

_____

_____

_____

_____

_____

_____

_____

_____

DAY ONE: LEARN IT

What type of things do you think about before going head to head with your competition?

_____

_____

_____

_____

_____

Vision - the act or power of anticipating that which will or may come to be. What vision do you have in mind when you go up against your competitor?

_____

_____

_____

_____

_____

_____

_____

_____

_____

having a vision is half the battle, strategizing is the other half.

DAY TWO: ACCEPT IT

Prepare a "Competitors' List." Identify your perceived competitors - people who are in a similar field and your real competitors - people who are actually doing what you are doing.

Perceived competitors	Real competitors

What vision do you have, when you think about going up against your perceived competitors vs. your real competitors? Is it different?

_____

_____

_____

_____

_____

_____

_____

_____

_____

YOU'VE GOT TO KNOW HOW MANY STEPS YOUR COMPETITORS ARE AHEAD OF YOU
You have to be precise and strategic to win the war!

DAY THREE: EMBRACE IT

Now that you know who your competitor is, research and identify what strategies your competitors use to make them successful

_____

_____

_____

_____

_____

_____

_____

_____

_____

_____

_____

_____

_____

_____

_____

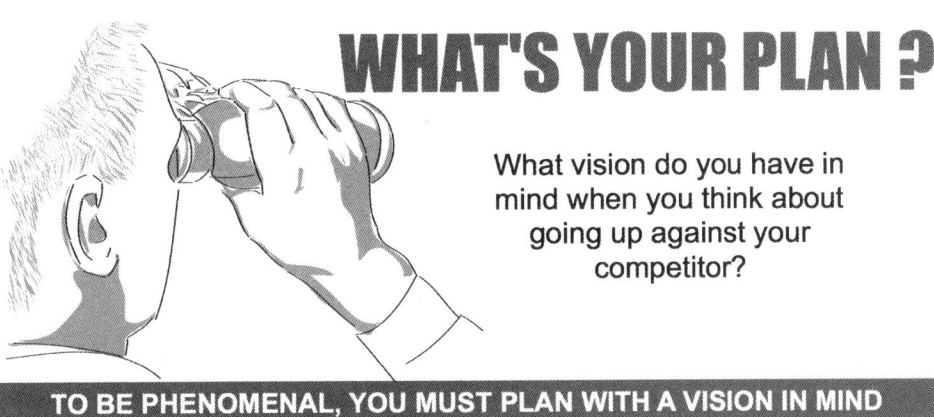

WHAT'S YOUR PLAN ?

What vision do you have in mind when you think about going up against your competitor?

TO BE PHENOMENAL, YOU MUST PLAN WITH A VISION IN MIND

DAY FOUR: CHANGE IT

Now that you have identified your competitor's success traits, determine which ones you need to incorporate and develop a strategy for how you will use this information to defeat your competition.

_____

_____

_____

_____

_____

_____

_____

_____

_____

DAY FIVE: LIVE IT

Now that you've identified your competition and your missing success traits, it's time to EXECUTE. Create a 7-day plan to describe what you will do to get ahead of the competition.

Sunday _____

_____

_____

_____

Monday _____

_____

_____

Tuesday _____

_____

_____

Wednesday _____

_____

_____

Thursday _____

_____

_____

Friday _____

_____

_____

Saturday _____

_____

_____

GREATNESS IS...

Howard Cosell said, "The ultimate victory in competition is derived from the inner satisfaction of knowing that you have done your best and that you have gotten the most out of what you had to give."

Listen, everybody has something special that they can bring to the table - a unique skill, creative energy, organization, well adapted social skills, etc. One of the greatest human attributes is our ability to be and express our uniqueness. But because we are all unique in our own rights, if you're looking to get ahead and stay ahead of your competition, you have to be willing to run that extra mile. You have to be willing to do what the next man wouldn't or couldn't because he was too distracted.

You can make it through the finish line; you can make it to the head of your class; you can become the new VP or COO of your company; you can manage your department; you can take your team to the

_____

playoffs; you can run circles around all of your competition, whomever they may be- but you've got to come to the table prepared.

The victory in competition isn't knowing that you won. Its knowing that when you were sitting at the table amongst the Greats, that you exhausted your talents and strengths to become the Greatest.

Greatness is realizing that the dividing line between you and your competition is how prepared you came to fight.

Spend time today reflecting on your actions this week.

Did you meet the challenge? If not, why?

_____

_____

_____

_____

_____

_____

_____

_____

_____

_____

_____

_____

_____

_____

_____

_____

_____

_____

_____

GIUY RE-UP
Weeks 5-7

Remember:

AVERAGE PEOPLE	GREATNESS...
Show an inability to prioritize their goals or responsibilities.	*Requires prioritizing.*
Believe that money is the only indicator of success.	*Requires investing in the interests of others.*
Don't invest in the interests of others.	*Requires building a Legacy.*
Forget their past and the things they had to experience to get where they are.	*Requires honoring debts owed to those people and neighborhoods shaped us.*
Are selfish.	*Requires selflessness.*
Feel entitled.	*Requires a willingness and eagerness to be of service to others.*
Express how entitled they are.	*Requires expressions of gratitude.*

Assess how well you've demonstrated your potential in this area on the scales below:

Before Reading

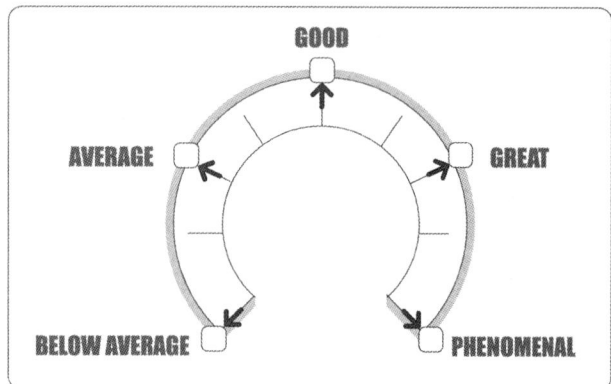

After Reading

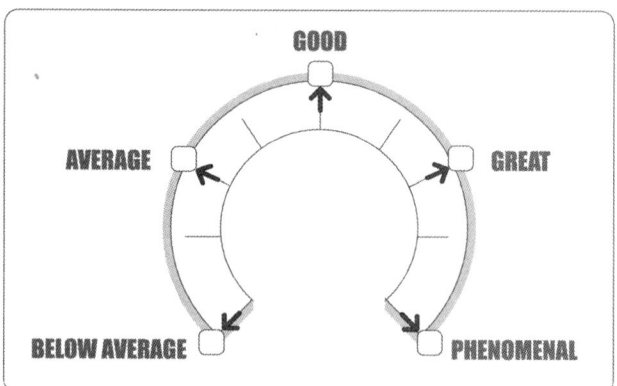

_____

_____

_____

_____

GREATNESS IS UPON YOU
CERTIFICATE OF COMPLETION

This is to certify that

_____

has successfully completed this week's challenge.

Eric Thomas and Associates, LLC

_____
signature

_____
date

WEEK 08
CURRENCY VS. LEGACY
GREATNESS PRINCIPLE #8:

Greatness is not taking for granted the lasting impact that giving to others can have on not just your life, but the lives of those you invested in.

Do you gauge success by how much money you obtain or by how many people you've managed to influence while you lived?

The next three chapters will discuss different aspects of service and its significance to your ability to obtain Greatness in all aspects of life. This week, we will focus on establishing longevity by investing in the lives of others.

What would building a Legacy mean for your family?

_____

_____

_____

_____

_____

_____

_____

_____

_____

_____

_____

_____

_____

_____

_____

_____

DAY ONE: LEARN IT

ARE YOU BUILDING A LEGACY OR COLLECTING CURRENCY?

Recall every time you worked for currency vs. Legacy, which one proved to be more rewarding in the long run?

What is the one thing you are working to achieve right now (i.e. set a new record, interview for a new program or position, etc.). How will that goal help you to create currency? How will it also help you to create a legacy?

currency	legacy

DAY TWO: ACCEPT IT
What can you do to make your time on earth memorable?

_____

_____

_____

_____

_____

_____

_____

DAY THREE: EMBRACE IT
What can you do to change the life of someone else with one simple act of kindness?

_____

_____

_____

_____

_____

_____

_____

_____

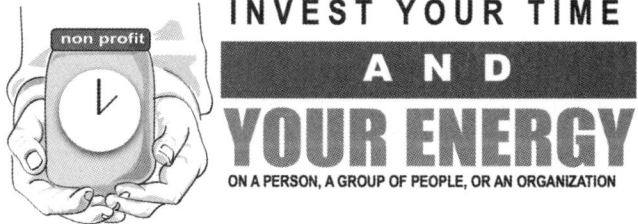

INVEST YOUR TIME
A N D
YOUR ENERGY
ON A PERSON, A GROUP OF PEOPLE, OR AN ORGANIZATION

Take the challenge:
What are the needs of the people in your community? Become a help in your community today by finding out how you can lend a hand (i.e. Soup Kitchen, Food Bank, etc.).

If possible, try volunteering at this location for 8 hours, in one month and record your experience below. How did your experience change your perspective or ideals about success?

Your experience _____

_____

_____

_____

_____

DAY FOUR: CHANGE IT

VISION

We discussed vision as it relates to getting a jump on your competitors in a previous chapter. But having a vision is equally important when trying to create a legacy.

STRATEGY/PLAN

How do you make your vision a reality? Who is involved? What will you need to get it going?

BUILD THE FOUNDATION

The truth is, everyone has something that they'll be remembered for, but that's not necessarily a good thing. You want to make sure that you're leaving behind something of value and, to do this, you must build your character. Revisit Week One.

ACCOUNTABILITY

Tell people about what you're doing and ask them to check in with you periodically. This is a good practice, even if it's only to remind you of the promises you made yourself.

What is the one thing that you can do today to begin your legacy?

_____

_____

_____

_____

_____

_____

_____

DAY FIVE: LIVE IT

Now that you know how to get started, create a 7-day plan to develop a legacy for yourself using the tools from Day Four.

Sunday _____

_____

_____

Monday _____

_____

_____

Tuesday _____

_____

_____

Wednesday _____

_____

_____

Thursday _____

_____

_____

Friday _____

_____

_____

Saturday _____

_____

_____

GREATNESS IS...

Marian Wright Edelman, President of the Children's Defense Fund said, "Never work just for money or for power. They won't save your soul or help you sleep at night."

Success is selfish. Just because you're successful doesn't mean that you're significant. Money does make you rich, but rich people die everyday failing to make a significant impact on the lives of the people who they had the chance to touch. The reality is that money, though necessary in many regards, is easily acquired and more easily spent. For this reason, there will always be somebody more educated, with more possessions and more money, to take their place. But when you're significant, people will always keep a place open for you. Mother Teresa, Martin Luther King Jr., and Ghandi may not have been business tycoons, but they were rich in what they gave because they enhanced the lives of others. Investing in the lives of others not only establishes longevity, it creates significance.

What will the headlines of the obituary say when it's your time to leave?

Greatness is not taking for granted the lasting impact that giving to others can have on not just your life, but the lives of those you invested in.

Spend time today reflecting on your actions this week.

Did you meet the challenge? If not, why?

_____

_____

_____

_____

_____

_____

_____

_____

_____

_____

_____

_____

_____

GREATNESS IS UPON YOU

CERTIFICATE OF COMPLETION

This is to certify that

_____

has successfully completed this week's challenge.

Eric Thomas and Associates, LLC

_____
signature

_____
date

WEEK 09
ALL ABOUT ME VS. RECIPROCITY
GREATNESS PRINCIPLE #9:

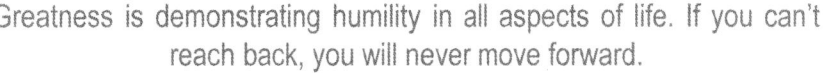

Greatness is demonstrating humility in all aspects of life. If you can't reach back, you will never move forward.

Do you live a life that says, "It's all about me" or does your life say, "I remember others"?

Don't just spend time seeking your own success or motivating and gaining inspiration for yourself; you increase your significance when you remember those who helped you get the process started.

Indicate whether these statements apply to you

☐	I call my family often just to say thank you for their support.
☐	I check in with my family and/or friends from my past just to see if I can help them with anything.
☐	I give those who helped me credit when I'm being applauded or praised for my success
☐	People often say things like, "I haven't heard from you..," "I never see you anymore...," or something similar.

If you checked either one of the statements above, write the reason below.

_____

_____

_____

_____

_____

_____

DAY ONE: LEARN IT

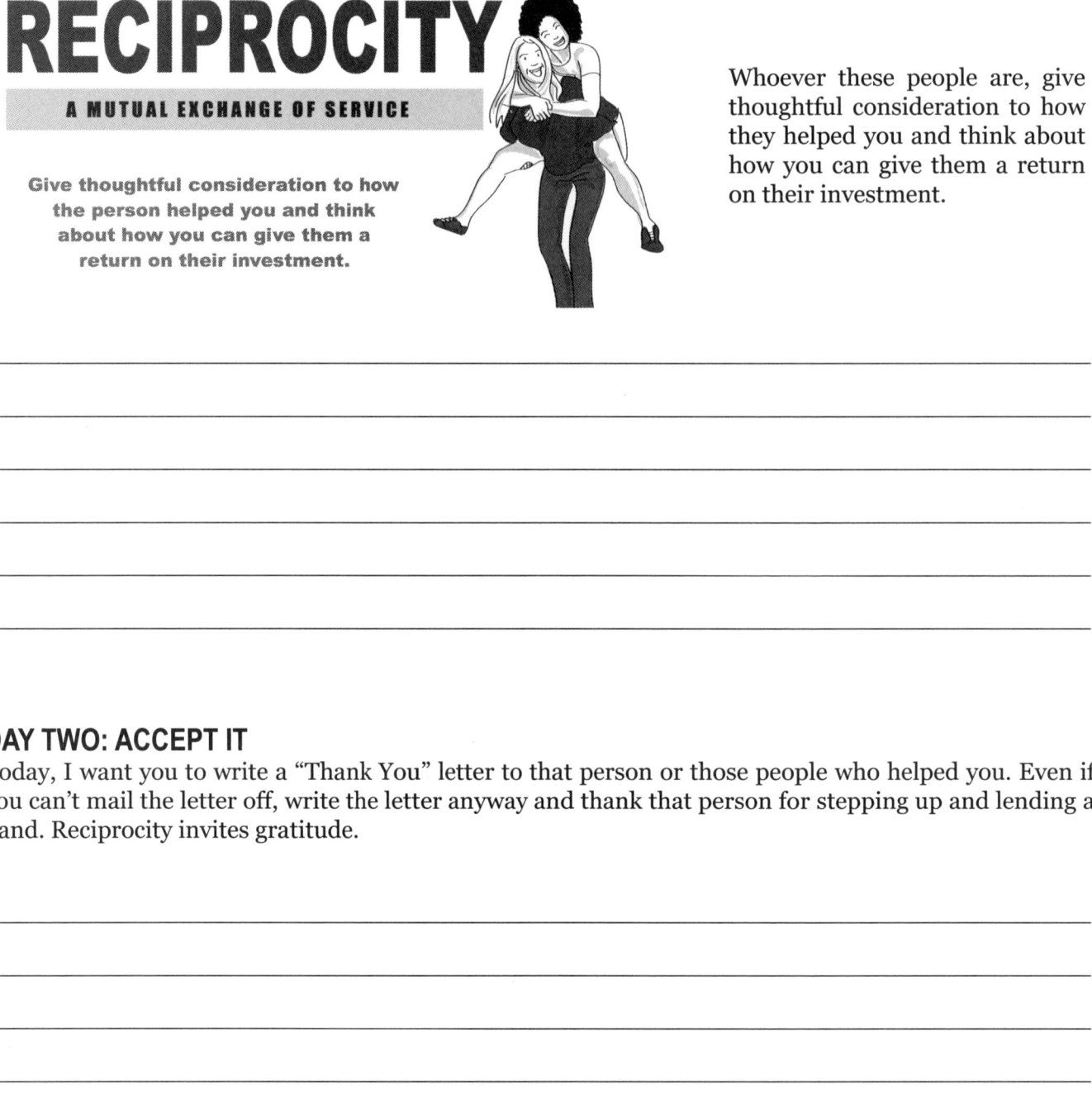

RECIPROCITY

A MUTUAL EXCHANGE OF SERVICE

Give thoughtful consideration to how the person helped you and think about how you can give them a return on their investment.

Whoever these people are, give thoughtful consideration to how they helped you and think about how you can give them a return on their investment.

_____

_____

_____

_____

_____

_____

DAY TWO: ACCEPT IT

Today, I want you to write a "Thank You" letter to that person or those people who helped you. Even if you can't mail the letter off, write the letter anyway and thank that person for stepping up and lending a hand. Reciprocity invites gratitude.

_____

_____

_____

_____

_____

_____

DAY THREE: EMBRACE IT

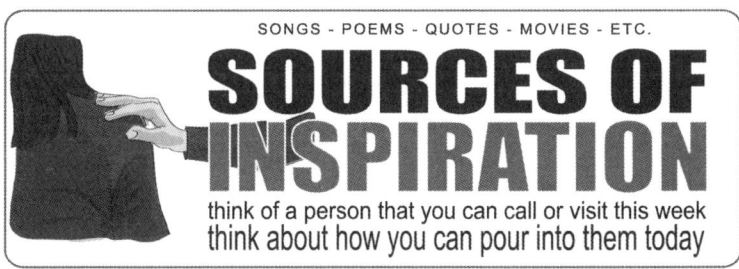

When was the last time you called your mom or dad just to give them something to help them through their day?

How often do you post or email an inspirational phrase or quote to your employee, boss, or a colleague who helped you meet your last deadline?

_____

_____

_____

_____

_____

_____

_____

_____

This morning, complete the following statements:

Today I commit to reaching out to _____

_____

_____   *I will share with him/her the following mo-*

tivational message: _____

_____

_____

Call and share with the person the reason you're sending the motivational message his or her way.

_____

DAY FOUR: CHANGE IT

SHARE YOUR INSPIRATIONS
LIFT THEIR SPIRIT

The goal is to physically show that person in a concrete way your gratitude and to simply convey the message: I remember you.

Today can be the day that you take another step towards Greatness. This week you've discovered gratitude in reciprocity and selfless inspiration. Now you're going to do or give something tangible to someone who helped you when you were low.

The goal is to physically show that person in a concrete way your gratitude and to simply convey the message: I remember you

What was this experience like?

_____

_____

_____

_____

_____

> *Life is like a riding a bicycle. To keep your balance, you must keep moving.*
> *- Albert Einstein*

DAY FIVE: LIVE IT

Create a 7-day plan that you can follow to give back to someone who helped you. This week you weren't able to get to everybody on that list, but who else do you need to reach out to? Be intentional about thinking about these people, and how you will reciprocate their investment.

Sunday _____

_____

_____

Monday _____

_____

_____

Tuesday _____

_____

_____

Wednesday _____

_____

_____

Thursday _____

_____

_____

Friday _____

_____

_____

Saturday _____

_____

_____

GREATNESS IS...

There is a parable about a Samaritan who stopped to help a man who had been attacked by robbers who left him half dead. The Samaritan bandaged his wounds, gave him food and drink, and made sure he was taken care of until he recovered. What would it say about the guy who was robbed, at a time in his life where he was at his best, if he were to see the Samaritan, now wounded and down on his luck, and not do anything to help him?

We should never forget those people who provided for us when we couldn't provide for ourself. But worse than forgetting, is remembering and doing nothing about it. Why? Because it shows a weakness in character that can only be described as selfish. And selfishness doesn't sustain success - it destroys it.

You didn't get to where you are in life because you deserve it, you got there because someone thought enough of you to give you a chance. Someone said, "Yes, I'll look out for you." "Yes, I believe in you," "Yes, I'll give you what you need." "Yes, I'll be there when you call me."

Greatness is demonstrating humility in all aspects of life. If you can't reach back, you will never move forward.

Spend time today reflecting on your actions this week.

Did you meet the challenge? If not, why?

GREATNESS IS UPON YOU

CERTIFICATE OF COMPLETION

This is to certify that

_____

has successfully completed this week's challenge.

Eric Thomas and Associates, LLC

_____
signature

_____
date

WEEK 10
ENTITLEMENT VS. LIFE OF SERVICE

Greatness Principle #10:
Greatness is understanding the importance of service and selfless acts as being necessary for the betterment of all mankind.

Do you view life in terms of what people owe you or in terms of what you can give back to people?

So far, we've discussed two aspects of Service: giving back to the people or cause that was instrumental in getting you started and giving others an opportunity to benefit from your success. This week we will discuss the distinction between service and entitlement.

How do you really view your life? You can speak in terms of what people owe you, in terms of what you can give back to other people, or perhaps its a mixture of both.

_____

_____

_____

_____

DAY ONE: LEARN IT

Identify 5 areas in your life where you function as though you have an entitled mindset. Meaning, your behavior says that the company you work for, your teachers, or anyone who you are involved in any type of relationship with owes you some benefit or award.

_____

_____

_____

_____

_____

_____

_____

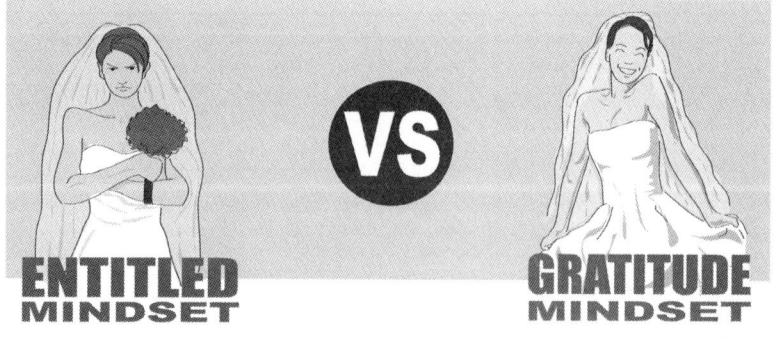

Identify 5 areas in your life where you function as though you have a mindset of service. Meaning, your behavior says that you are grateful and willing to do whatever is necessary to see a positive end result.

_____

_____

_____

_____

_____

_____

_____

DAY TWO: ACCEPT IT

Yesterday, you identified areas in your life where you felt entitled and areas in your life where you expressed gratitude. Today, you are going to accept which behavior you identify more with when it comes to your approach in life.

ENTITLEMENT MINDSET

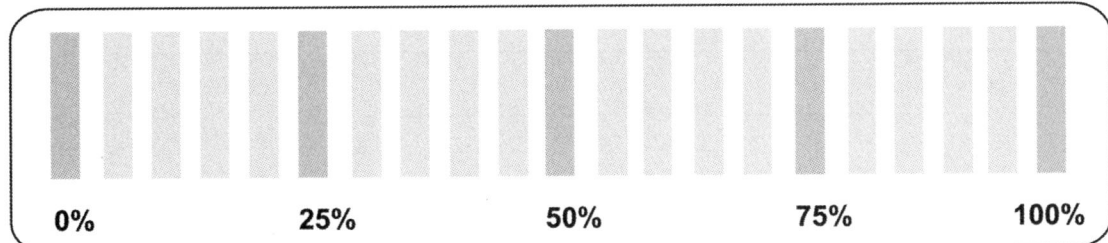

- 0% -I never feel like anyone owes me anything.
- 25%-I rarely feel like anyone owes me anything.
- 50%- I sometimes feel like I'm entitled to certain benefits or rewards.
- 75%- Many times, I feel like its my right to have certain benefits or rewards.
- 100% - I always feel like I'm entitled to certain benefits or rewards.

GRATITUDE MINDSET

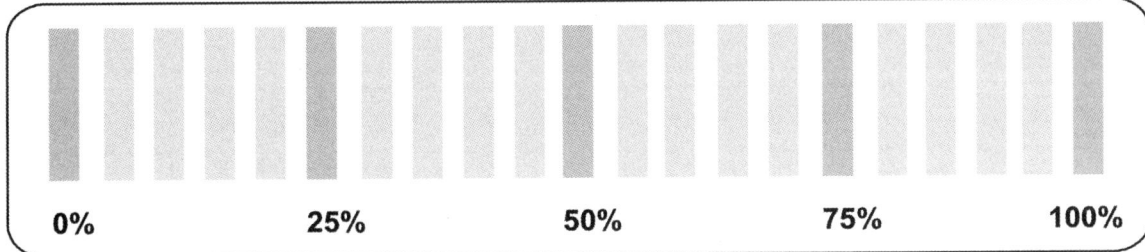

- 0%- I never behave in a spirit of gratitude and service to others.
- 25%- I rarely behave in a spirit of gratitude and service to others.
- 50% - I sometimes behave in a spirit of gratitude and service to others.
- 75%-Most times I behave in a spirit of gratitude and service to others.
- 100% - I always behave in a spirit of gratitude and service to others.

Which behavior did you identify more with? Why did you give it the percentage ranking that you did?

_____

_____

_____

_____

_____

DAY THREE: EMBRACE IT

Today, you are going to get more specific about areas in your life where you feel a false sense of entitlement.

I expect _____

_____

even when I _____

_____

_____

_____

_____

I expect _____

_____

even when I _____

_____

_____

_____

_____

I expect _____

_____

even when I _____

_____

_____

_____

_____

GOT TO DO GET TO DO

WHAT SIDE OF THE SPECTRUM CONSUMES MORE OF YOUR LIFE?

DAY FOUR: CHANGE IT

Think about 3 times in your life, where you "Got" to do something, and you took it for granted. For example: "I've 'Got' to take my kids to school before I go to work," as opposed to "I 'Get' to take my kids to school before I go to work."

_____

_____

_____

_____

_____

_____

What does your behavior look like in these situations? How do people respond to your behavior, and is that the response that will help you to live your fullest life?

_____

_____

_____

_____

_____

_____

_____

DAY FIVE: LIVE IT

Draft your 7-day plan to live a life that is based more on those things you "get to do" and not "got to do."

Sunday _____

_____

_____

Monday _____

_____

_____

Tuesday _____

_____

_____

Wednesday _____

_____

_____

Thursday _____

_____

_____

Friday _____

_____

_____

Saturday _____

_____

_____

GREATNESS IS...

A while ago, someone emailed me a story about a little girl during the Depression. In the story, the little girl went to the store with her mom, and when they walked out of the store and walked up the street a few blocks, the little girl saw some imitation pearl earrings in one of the store windows for $2. At that time, $2 was a lot of money, so her mom told her that they couldn't afford it at that moment but reminded her of her grandma's yearly Christmas gift of $1. She told her daughter that if she did a few chores, she would give her the other dollar she needed.

The little girl gets so excited and immediately sets out to do as many chores as she could and eventually collects a $1 bill from her grandma and her mother. As anticipated, the little girl buys the pearls, and she wears them everywhere; she literally wore them every where she went. She wore them to school, to church, to bed, in the bathtub...she loved them so much that she would never take them off.

One day her dad comes to her and asks her if he can have the pearls. This devastated the little girl because, even though she loved her father, she had worked hard to get her pearls and had no desire to let them go. So she tried to bargain with him and offered to give him her new baby doll with the pink pony instead. Her father declined.

About a month later, her dad came back again and asked his daughter, "Do you love me?"

"Yes, Dad, I love you," she said.

"Do you really love me?" he asked.

"Yes, Dad. I really love you," she told him.

"Ok. Do this for me. Let me have those two pearl earrings," he said.

"Daddy, I love you, but...I can't give you these pearl earrings, Daddy. I worked hard for them and Grandma gave me the extra dollar," she said.

The dad said, "Ok," and kissed her goodnight.

Two weeks later, her dad came home, and she was sitting in the living room shaking and crying. Her dad asked, "Baby, what's wrong?" She said, "Daddy, you remember when you asked me for the pearls?" "Yes, I remember," he answered.

The little girl stood up, reached for her daddy's hand and said, "Daddy, I love you." The little girl placed the pearls in her daddy's hand.

And while she was giving her father the pearls, he began to smile and he took the pearls with his left hand, but with his right hand he pulled out a velvet box. He handed the box to his daughter and told her to open it.

The little girl opened the box and a tear began to fall down her cheek. The father, showing his daughter the two fake pearl earrings in his left hand, asked, "Do you remember when I first asked you for these?"

The little girl nodded, "Yes."

"Well, I had these waiting for you the whole time," the father said as he reached into the velvet box and pulled out a genuine pearl necklace and placed it around his daughter's neck. "But because you weren't willing to give me those, I couldn't give you the real thing."

The moral of the story is that she wasn't willing to give up what she had not knowing that if she had given those things up that she had something better coming. Some of you will never be able to get on that next level, because there are some things that you're just not willing to let go of (i.e., your time, your energy, your talent, your money) because you feel like you've earned it, or you've forgotten where you came from, or are too consumed with stabilizing your financial status. At any given moment anyone else could be in your shoes, doing your job, building your home, loving your friends. But somehow, they chose you. Your boss chose you; your mate chose you; your friends chose you. Never forget that it wasn't you, but mercy and grace that is responsible for you being where you are.

Greatness is understanding the importance of service and selfless acts as being necessary for the betterment of all mankind.

Spend time today reflecting on your actions this week.

Did you meet the challenge? If not, why?

_____

_____

_____

_____

_____

_____

_____

_____

_____

_____

_____

_____

GIUY RE-UP
Weeks 8-10

REMEMBER:

AVERAGE PEOPLE	GREATNESS...
Believe that money is the only indicator of success.	*Requires investing in to the interests of others.*
Don't invest in the interests of others.	*Requires building a Legacy.*
Forget their past and the things they had to experience to get where they are.	*Requires honoring debts owed to those people and neighborhoods that shaped us.*
Are selfish.	*Requires selflessness.*
Feel entitled.	*Requires a willingness and eagerness to be of service to others.*
Express how entitled they are.	*Requires expressions of gratitude.*

Assess how well you've demonstrated your potential in this area on the scales below:

Before Reading :

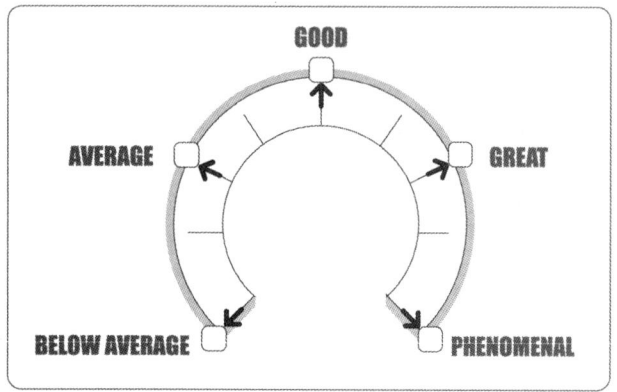

After Reading :

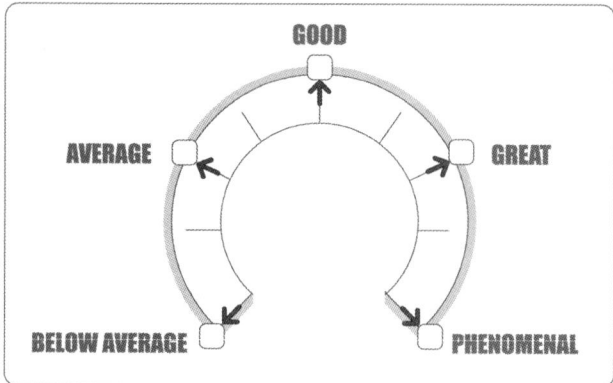

GREATNESS IS UPON YOU
CERTIFICATE OF COMPLETION

This is to certify that

_____

has successfully completed this week's challenge.

Eric Thomas and Associates, LLC

_____
signature

_____
date

WEEK 11
LURKER VS. HUNTER - ROUND 1
GREATNESS PRINCIPLE #11:

Greatness is moving outside of your comfort zone, because out of your comfort zone is where the miracles happen. If it doesn't challenge you, it won't change you.

Are you waiting for your next meal or are you going out to catch it?

Early in my career, I had to learn that I wasn't getting as far as I wanted to go because I was complacent - I had characteristics of the lurking Crocodile:

How does complacency threaten your personal or professional growth?

_____

_____

_____

_____

_____

_____

_____

_____

_____

_____

_____

_____

_____

_____

_____

_____

LEARN IT

In the space provided below, address what area in your life the Lurker's mindset is active in. Then address how this mentality has hindered your growth.

I probably have a "Lurker's" mentality because ... _____

_____

_____

_____

_____

How has this mentality hindered Your growth?

_____

_____

_____

_____

_____

_____

_____

THE LURKING CROCODILE

Crocodiles can sit and wait for days for an opportunity to eat ...

WHAT ARE YOU WAITING FOR ?

ACCEPT IT

What opportunities are you waiting on? What opportunities have you taken advantage of and then became satisfied? Why is that?

I accept that I am presently waiting on the following opportunities :

_____

_____

_____

_____

_____

I accept that I took advantage of the following opportunities but became satisfied once I achieved:

_____

_____

_____

_____

_____

Identify areas in your life where you have failed to take initiative and, as a result, missed a golden opportunity.

How has that hindered the growth of your company or the people you work with?

_____

_____

_____

_____

EMBRACE IT

Lurkers perceive time as though it lasts forever. Like the circular clock above, time is never ending for them.

When you move from the perspective of the hour glass, every second counts - you don't have time to spare.

Waiting takes time. We miss out on so many opportunities simply because they're not within our immediate reach.

_____

_____

_____

_____

_____

Which time piece do you operate from?

_____

_____

_____

What concrete examples can you pull from to support your answer?

_____

_____

_____

_____

CHANGE IT

Using the information you wrote about in the "Embrace It" exercise, write about how you can aggressively seek out each opportunity you're lurking for. Pair each moment you're waiting on with the appropriate aggressive attack.

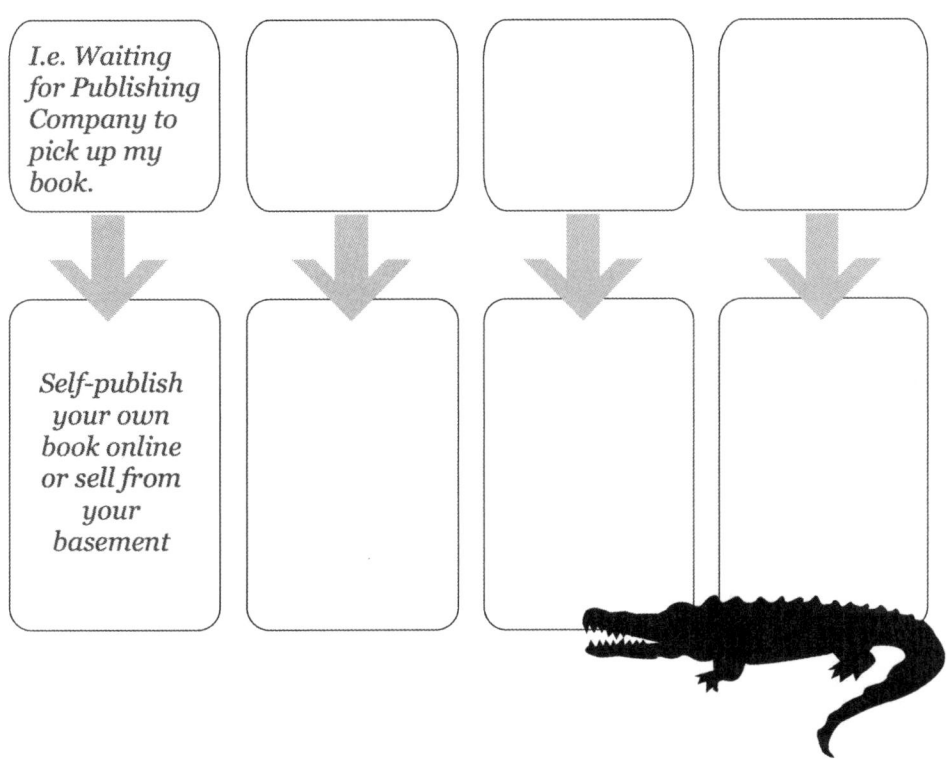

LIVE IT

Create a 7-day plan to get rid of your Lurker's Mentality.

Sunday _____

_____

_____

Monday _____

_____

_____

Tuesday _____

_____

_____

Wednesday _____

_____

_____

Thursday _____

_____

_____

Friday _____

_____

_____

Saturday _____

_____

_____

GREATNESS IS...

There was a King who was unlike any other king the people had heard of because He didn't live in a castle, He didn't wear the fancy clothes, and He didn't use his power in the traditional sense. But what He had, which piqued the curiosity of the people in his city, was the ability to change lives. So he walked the streets of city after city, teaching and healing those He would encounter and as word got around of His presence and the incredible things He was doing for the people, multitudes began to follow Him because they wanted to know and understand more and they wanted to be healed.

The King, seeing the crowd, decided to walk up a mountain. As He journeyed, the multitudes of people who were just moments earlier, following the King, asking and begging for more information and more healing, remained behind and watched Him as He made his move up the mount. The King sat on the mountain knowing that only those who really wanted the wisdom He was getting ready to share would be willing and courageous enough to follow Him; the others would remain behind and wait for those who received the wisdom to bring the information back down the mountain. Some of them would do this because they were afraid to make the sacrifice of climbing the mountain, some of them stayed behind because they were content with just being in the atmosphere, some of them were too needy and insecure to take the hike, some of them weren't there to get information at all but just wanted to be seen with the crowd, and others of them knew that if they waited long enough, someone else would go and get what was needed and bring it down to the rest of them. When the King took His seat, only twelve of His followers came to Him - the King never called for them or tried to get their attention, they just came. And the King taught them as people of authority and not as mere scribes.

Which group would you have been a part of? Would you have been one of the twelve or a part of the

_____

remaining multitude?

Greatness is moving outside of your comfort zone, because out of your comfort zone is where the miracles happen. If it doesn't challenge you, it won't change you.

Spend time today reflecting on your actions this week.

Did you meet the challenge? If not, why?

_____

_____

_____

_____

_____

_____

_____

_____

_____

_____

_____

_____

_____

_____

_____

_____

_____

_____

_____

_____

GREATNESS IS UPON YOU
CERTIFICATE OF COMPLETION

This is to certify that

_____

has successfully completed this week's challenge.

Eric Thomas and Associates, LLC

_____
signature

_____
date

WEEK 12
LURKER VS. HUNTER - ROUND 2
GREATNESS PRINCIPLE #12:
Greatness is deciding to take action, not just for your life, but for the lives of those who depend on you.

Does your behavior say "I'm driven" or "I'm content"?

What really drives you and gets you moving? Remember, Lurkers sit and wait, but if you're really going to get ahead, there are some opportunities you're going to have to get up and take.

When I go to work, I clock in and watch the clock the whole day, eager to clock out.	☐ True	☐ False
I often say things like, "When the time is right," or "I'm waiting for the right moment."	☐ True	☐ False
I believe that anything having in life is worth going after.	☐ True	☐ False
I believe that if you wait long enough, the right opportunities will come to you.	☐ True	☐ False

Based off of your answers above, does your behavior say "I'm driven" or "I'm content?"

_____

_____

_____

_____

_____

_____

_____

_____

_____

LEARN IT

THE LURKER (Crocodile)   or   THE HUNTER (Bear)

When it comes to your career, school, or your personal life, who do you identify more with, the Lurker (Crocodile) or the Hunter (Bear)?

Lurker	Hunter
Wait for opportunities to come to them.	*Looks for opportunities or creates his or her own.*
Becomes complacent after seizing an opportunity.	*Is never satisfied.*
Waits for the right moment to "strike" from fear of a missed opportunity.	*Takes Action: "All In" or nothing at all*

Who do you have in your life who would stand to benefit from your having a Hunter's Mentality?

_____

_____

_____

_____

_____

What have you lost by allowing yourself to behave like a Lurker? You may use your answer(s) from last week.

_____

_____

_____

_____

_____

ACCEPT AND EMBRACE IT

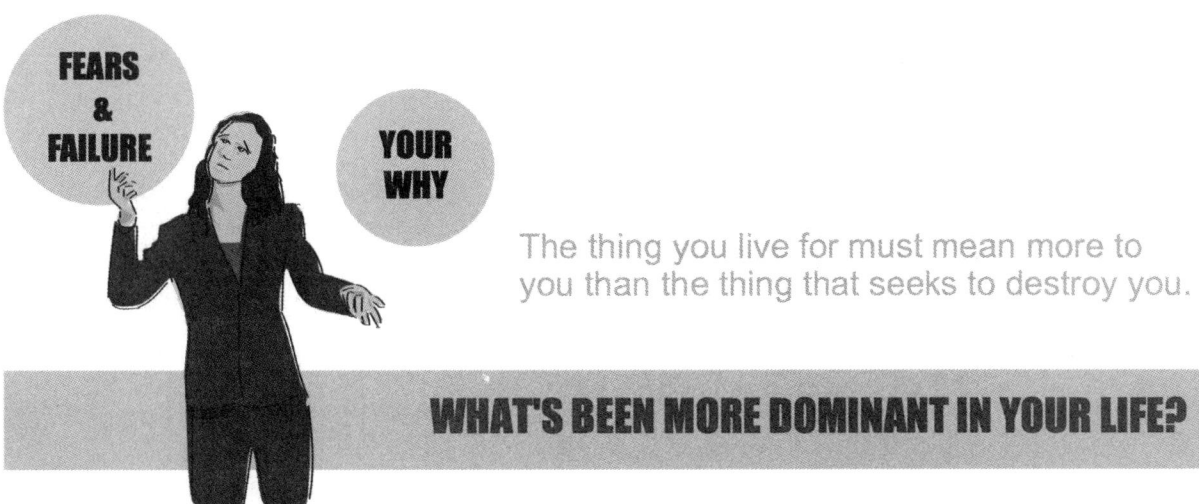

The thing you live for must mean more to you than the thing that seeks to destroy you.

WHAT'S BEEN MORE DOMINANT IN YOUR LIFE?

What's been more dominant in your life, your fears and failures or your Purpose?

_____

_____

_____

_____

What drives you?

_____

_____

_____

_____

_____

_____

_____

_____

_____

_____

_____

How to develop a Hunter's Mentality.

In the speedometers below, indicate where you stand in terms of your drive in each of the areas listed. Don't just rate yourself in these areas. Take time to consider why you scored yourself the way that you did. For instance, if you give yourself an 8 in terms of your drive to be focused on your goals, then think about the reasons why you aren't a 10. Have you always been an 8?

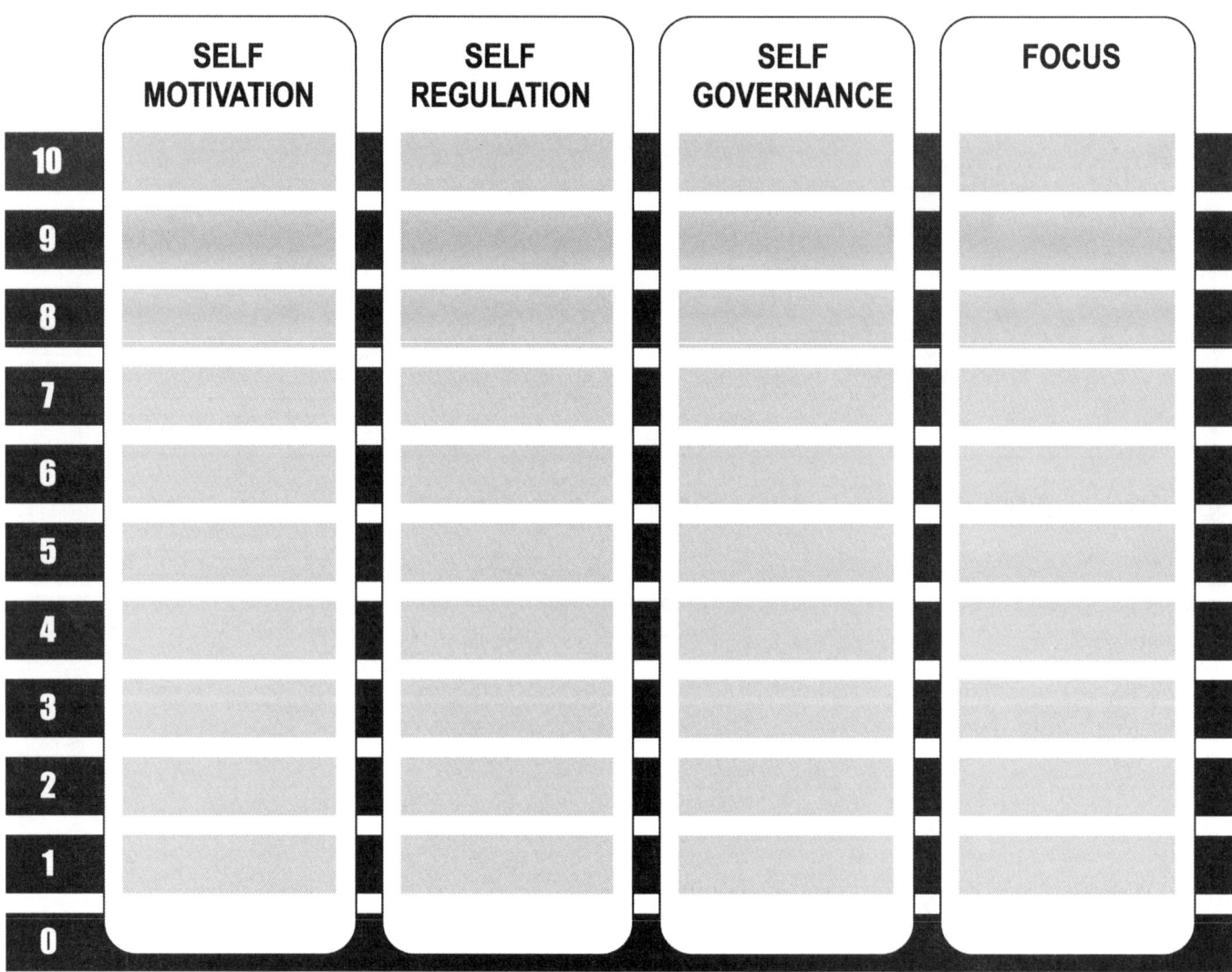

1. **Self-regulation** - Learn to Discipline yourself

What was your rank? _____

*Why?*_____

_____

How could you be better? _____

_____

2. **Self-motivation** - Don't wait for others to motivate you.

What was your rank? _____

*Why?*_____

_____

*How could you be better?*_____

_____

3. **Self-governance** - Make your own decisions.

What was your rank? _____

*Why?*_____

_____

*How could you be better?*_____

_____

4. **Focus** - Your goals should be your focal point.

What was your rank? _____

*Why?*_____

_____

*How could you be better?*_____

_____

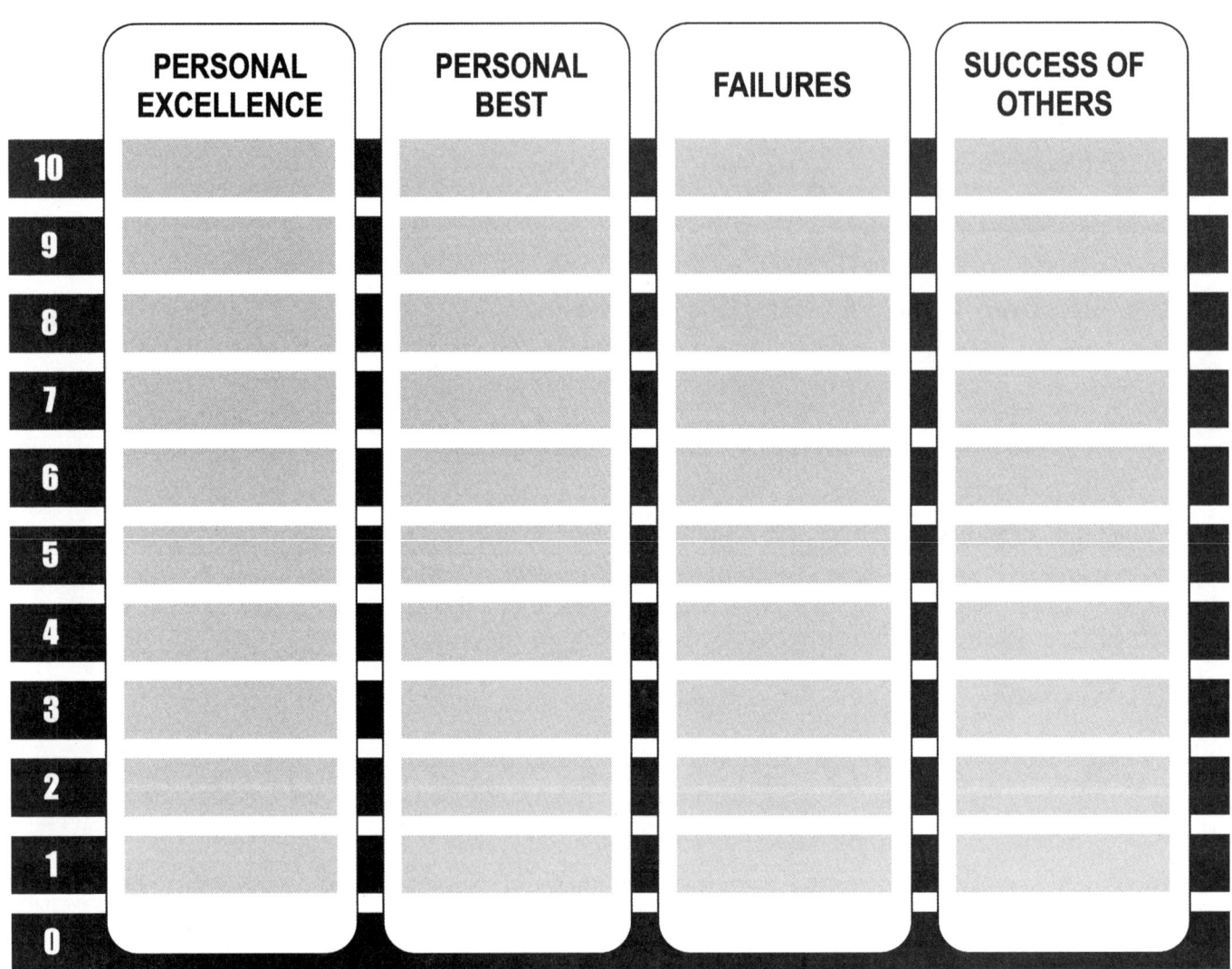

5. **Personal Excellence** - Commit to performing a task that you want to represent you.

What was your rank? _____

*Why?*_____

_____

How could you be better? _____

_____

6. **Personal Best** - You're only as good as you can be.

What was your rank? _____

*Why?*_____

_____

How could you be better? _____

_____

7. **Failures** - Failing isn't the part the matters, refusing to get up makes you a failure.

What was your rank? _____

*Why?*_____

_____

How could you be better? _____

_____

8. **The success of others** - Use others success as motivation, not as discouragement.

What was your rank? _____

*Why?*_____

_____

How could you be better? _____

_____

Think about the eight ways to develop a Hunter's Mentality, and write down your thoughts, and plans to make them a reality.

_____

_____

_____

_____

_____

_____

_____

_____

_____

_____

Allow your passion to become your purpose, and it will one day become your profession.
- Gabrielle Bernstein

CHANGE IT

List the top 10 most destructive habits that are suffocating your drive and hindering your Hunter's Mindset. What's keeping you from getting to where you need to be at this point in your life?

1. _____

_____

2. _____

_____

3. _____

_____

4. _____

_____

5. _____

_____

6. _____

_____

7. _____

_____

8. _____

_____

9. _____

_____

10. _____

_____

PUSH YOURSELF FROM WITHIN

Push your self from within: What can you let go of today to help you score a 10 in each area?

1. _____

2. _____

3. _____

4. _____

5. _____

6. _____

7. _____

8. _____

9. _____

10. _____

Think about 3 to 5 ways the information from the Accept It/Embrace It activity can revolutionize your thinking and shift your behavior.

1. _____
_____

2. _____
_____

3. _____
_____

4. _____
_____

5. _____
_____

LIVE IT
Now that you know what intensifies your drive and the obstacles that hinder your drive and, in turn, your ability to hunt, create a 7-day plan to help you stay on track to having a Hunter's Mentality.

_____

Sunday _____

_____

_____

Monday _____

_____

_____

Tuesday _____

_____

_____

Wednesday _____

_____

_____

Thursday _____

_____

_____

Friday _____

_____

_____

Saturday _____

_____

_____

GREATNESS IS...

"Do something."

These two words, in my opinion, are the most powerful words in the movie, John Q. I've watched a few movies in my day and none have moved me in the way that John Q has. Every time I think about taking *a day off or not being productive in some fashion, I remember that scene where Denzel's wife looks at him after finding out that their son only has hours to live, and she says those two words.*

In two words, she conveyed what it means to be a Hunter: take action. And because of this, her husband, who at one point was waiting for things to happen, experiences a shift in mentality and seeks out a means to get things done. I am not saying that his actions should be duplicated, but I am saying that the mind shift from Lurker to Hunter was captivating, because it sends the message that even if you are a Lurker in most aspects of your life, when given the proper motivation, you have the power to go out and hunt.

What if your son, daughter, or someone really significant in your life needed something that was life changing and all that was required of you was to focus in a way that you have never focused before... no snooze button and no extra day off? What if their well- being or your ability to increase the quality of your own life was predicated on your performance? What shift is going to have to happen in your life for you to take action?What needs to happen to get you to stop hitting the snooze button?

Greatness is deciding to take action, not just for your life, but for the lives of those who depend on you.

Spend time today reflecting on your actions this week.

Did you meet the challenge? If not, why?

_____

_____

_____

_____

_____

_____

_____

_____

_____

_____

_____

_____

_____

GREATNESS IS UPON YOU

GREATNESS IS UPON YOU

CERTIFICATE OF COMPLETION

This is to certify that

_____

has successfully completed this week's challenge.

Eric Thomas and Associates, LLC

_____
signature

_____
date

WEEK 13
LURKER VS. HUNTER - ROUND 3

GREATNESS PRINCIPLE #13:

Greatness is valuing the rewards of a mutual relationship over selfish ambition.

How do you get along with the opposing forces of the Jungle?

You may realize that you're a Lurker but need some time to transition from that mindset; in the meantime, how do you function in an office with a Bear? Or perhaps you mostly function as a Hunter but find yourself frustrated by the complacency of the Crocodiles in your environment and need to understand how to cope better. This week we take a deeper look at the different type of relationships that can exist between the Crocodile and the Bear in the office.

Check the ONE that is most applicable to you.

☐	I think that it's important to get all you can out of life, no matter how it affects other people.
☐	I think that it's important to get all you can out of life as long as it doesn't harm other people.
☐	I think that it's important to get all you want out of life and I do my best to make sure that others can do the same.

Why do you hold this belief?

_____

_____

_____

_____

_____

_____

_____

_____

_____

_____

LEARN IT

List your Office Behaviors, Family/Social Behaviors, and Personal Behaviors in the appropriate places to the right.

PARASITISM

COMMENSALISM

MUTUALISM

	Which area did most of your behaviors fall in?
HOMELESS / HIGH SCHOOL DROP OUT / INTERNATIONAL MOTIVATIONAL TEACHER / 12 YEARS TO GET A 4 YEAR DEGREE	

ACCEPT IT
What are you doing in your work environment to cause you to relate to that group? Be specific.

_____

_____

_____

_____

_____

_____

_____

Have you ever been part of a situation in which you didn't help or hurt the progression? What was your role?

_____

_____

_____

_____

_____

_____

_____

EMBRACE IT

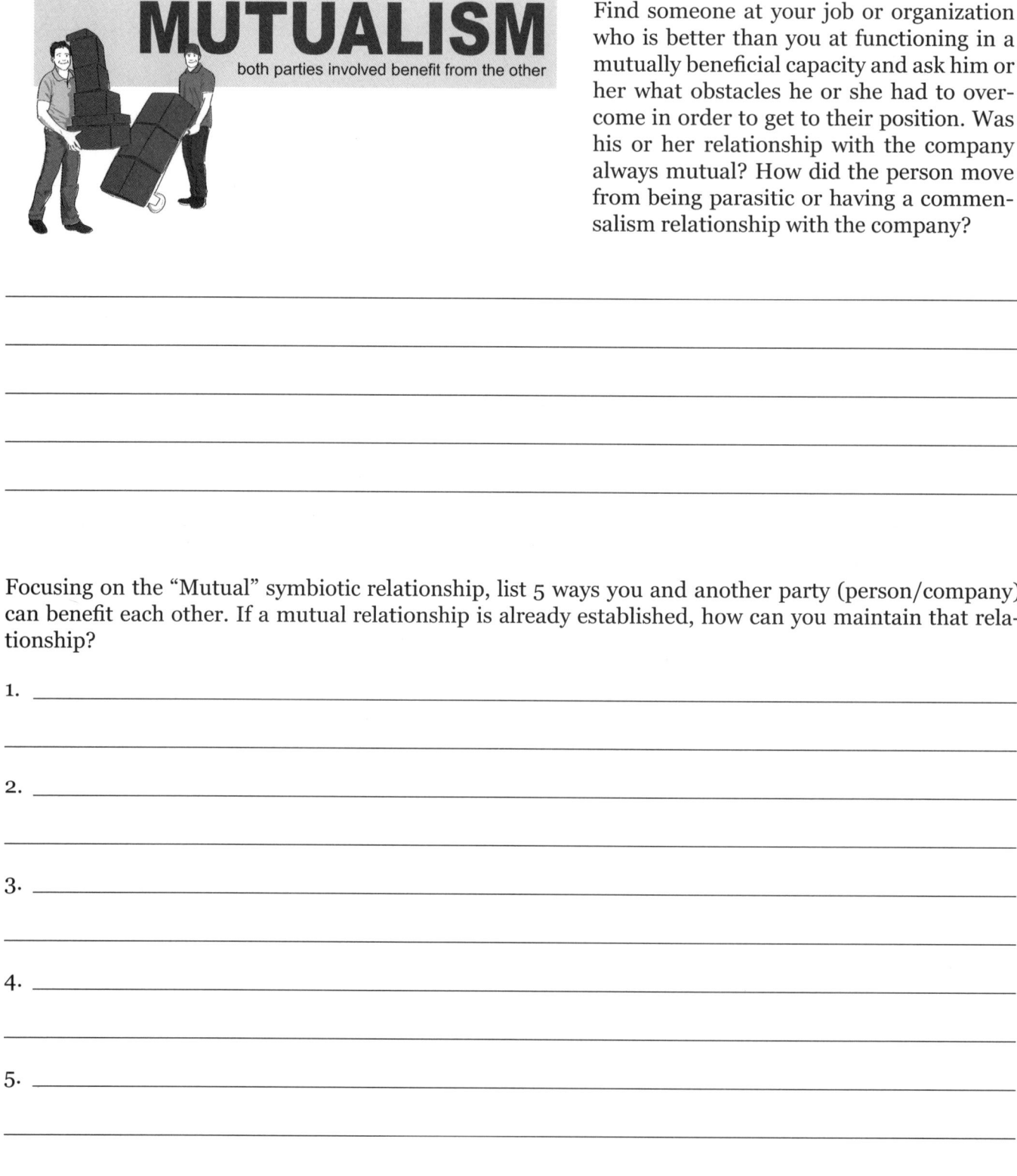

MUTUALISM
both parties involved benefit from the other

Find someone at your job or organization who is better than you at functioning in a mutually beneficial capacity and ask him or her what obstacles he or she had to overcome in order to get to their position. Was his or her relationship with the company always mutual? How did the person move from being parasitic or having a commensalism relationship with the company?

_____

_____

_____

_____

_____

Focusing on the "Mutual" symbiotic relationship, list 5 ways you and another party (person/company) can benefit each other. If a mutual relationship is already established, how can you maintain that relationship?

1. _____

_____

2. _____

_____

3. _____

_____

4. _____

_____

5. _____

_____

CHANGE IT

Recite the following:

"I know that I am able to have a mutually beneficial relationship within my company or organization. I can do the following things to accomplish this goal (i.e., come to work, take an appropriate length lunch break, etc.)":

_____

_____

_____

_____

_____

PARASITISM
one organism benefits and the other organism is harmed

Identify your behaviors that contribute to a more parasitic relationship.

_____

_____

_____

_____

_____

LIVE IT

Remember, mutual relationships benefit both parties involved. Profits and productivity are maximized when employees feel that they are getting the most out of their careers (i.e., salaries, benefits, growth opportunities, etc.) and CEOs feel that they are getting the most out of their investment in the employees' skills, talents, and potential. Create a 7-day plan that you will use to help you to move toward a stronger mutual relationship between you and your company or organization.

Sunday _____

_____

_____

Monday _____

_____

_____

Tuesday _____

_____

_____

Wednesday _____

_____

_____

Thursday _____

_____

_____

Friday _____

_____

_____

Saturday _____

_____

_____

_____

GREATNESS IS...

There's a story of a man who was once the Judge over a whole nation and, because of his physical strength, was able to single handedly defeat his nation's enemies one by one. The mystery behind his strength was one of grave concern to the enemy camp. They knew that if they could find his weakness, they would be able to overtake him, and such would end his reign over his Nation.

When the enemies learned of the Judge's affair with a woman in a neighboring village, they saw this as an opportunity to get the information they needed to bring about the Judge's demise. They offered the woman a large sum of money to join their scheme to uncover the secret to the Judge's great strength.

Weak in his affection towards the woman, the Judge eventually gave in to her persistent requests to know what made him so powerful. He confessed that the secret to his strength was in his hair - he took a vow at birth that his hair would never be touched.

Later that night, while asleep, the woman called out for her coconspirators. She told them the Judge's secret, and they shaved off his hair and bound him. Now weak and defenseless, the Judge was captured and the Nation that he had spent his life trying to protect, was left vulnerable to the attacks of their enemy.

Listen, things didn't fall apart for the Judge because he fell in love, and it didn't fall apart simply because he allowed himself to trust someone. The issue developed when he attached himself to a relationship that was one sided. When we aren't aware of the nature of our relationships, we put ourselves in the position to not only be deceived but to be destroyed. He allowed himself to connect with someone who cared more about what she could get out of him than what she could give him. She didn't care about his goals and dreams or even his safety. She was the ultimate parasite.

Our feelings, our desire to make money, our desire to avoid hurting others' feelings, our need to get out of uncomfortable situations, etc. can function to not only blind us to the true nature of people, they are also the reasons why we sometimes latch on to relationships (personal and professional) in a way that can be detrimental. You don't want to be the parasite any more than you want to be the victim of the parasite.

Greatness is valuing the rewards of a mutual relationship over selfish ambition.

Spend time today reflecting on your actions this week.

Did you meet the challenge? If not, why?

_____

_____

_____

_____

_____

GIUY RE-UP

In Summary, when it comes to being a Lurker vs. Hunter...

AVERAGE PEOPLE	GREATNESS...
Wait for opportunities to come to them.	*Requires a hunger satisfied through the hunt.*
Are satisfied.	*Requires a constant hunger.*
Can wait extended lengths of time for the next "big" opportunity.	*Requires an ability to shift environments.*
Foster relationships that are either parasitic or commensalistic in nature.	*Requires relationships that are mutualistic in nature.*

Assess how well you've demonstrated your potential in this area on the scales below:

Before Reading :

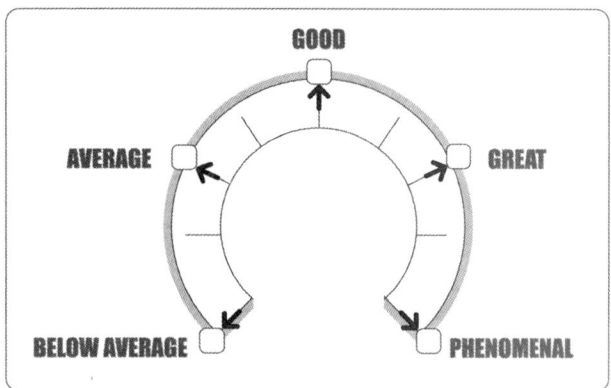

After Reading :

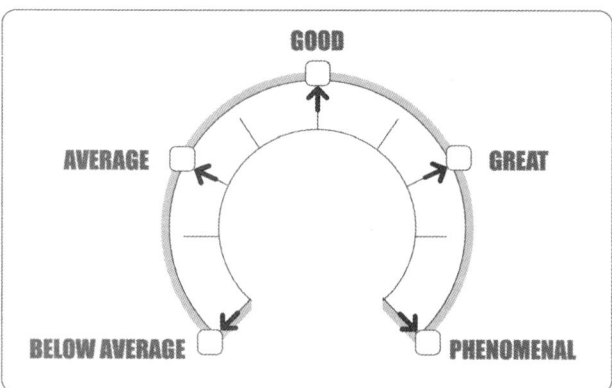

GREATNESS IS UPON YOU
CERTIFICATE OF COMPLETION

This is to certify that

_____

has successfully completed this week's challenge.

Eric Thomas and Associates, LLC

_____
signature

_____
date

WEEK 14
SINK VS. SWIM
GREATNESS PRINCIPLE #14:
Greatness is acknowledging that as talented and successful as you may be, there is someone else who can show you more.

Do you behave as though you've already learned all that you need to learn or are you open to new information?

Having a mentor is a great step in facilitating your personal and professional development. The concept of having a Mentor goes all the way back to Plato and Socrates. Mentors are a great resource to new information and potentially golden gateways to success, because if you pay attention to them, you not only gain a wealth of information, but you also get to learn from their mistakes.

Have you ever had an encounter with a "Know It All?" At work? At school? At home? Think about the last time you were face to face with someone who thought that they knew everything. What were your thoughts? What affect did their energy have on the other people in their environment? Has that person ever been You? How do you know?

_____

_____

_____

_____

_____

_____

_____

_____

_____

_____

_____

_____

_____

_____

HAVING A MENTOR
a great step in facilitating your personal and professional development.

LEARN IT
What steps are you taking to stretch yourself?

_____

_____

_____

_____

_____

Recognize.
Name 3 people that you view as mentors in your life. Next to their name, explain what key attributes they exhibit that make them qualified to be your mentor.

1. _____

_____

_____

2. _____

_____

_____

3. _____

_____

_____

Research.

Write down books, magazines, websites, and blogs that will help you relate to your mentor. (The ability to hold a conversation can take you far!)

_____

_____

_____

_____

_____

_____

EMBRACE IT

Ask.

Use these questions to help you get started when speaking with your mentor. Take notes, and come up with your own as the conversation progresses.

How did you accomplish your goal?

_____

_____

_____

_____

_____

What road did you take?

_____

_____

_____

_____

_____

_____

What were the challenges and how did you overcome them?

_____

_____

_____

_____

_____

_____

ACCEPT IT

Repeat this phrase out loud three times: I'm good at what I do, but I don't know everything.
Now, fill in the blanks below.

*I am very skilled a*_____ *t*

_____

and _____

_____

Even so, I accept the fact that I don't know all there is to know about these areas, and I understand that there are others who know more and who may be better at them than me.

Before you can begin to move in the direction of

GROWTH

there may be some things that you have to let go of to get started

Before you can begin to move in the direction of growth, there may be some things that you have to let go of to get started. For example, pride, arrogance, or an inflated ego are popular obstacles that get in the way of a person being able to seek out other sources for help.

Accepting this does not make you less of a person nor does it lessen your abilities.

I will let go of the following things: _____

_____

_____

_____

and _____

_____

to help myself grow in these areas. _____

_____

_____

_____

CHANGE IT

Today, we're going to deal with the positive, but before we journey there take a look at the diagram below. Assess where you fall on the Guru-Meter.

- A Novice is still getting to know his craft; he may perform well in it but still has a lot to learn.
- A Master knows his craft very well, but he is not able to teach it to others for the purpose of duplication.
- An Expert not only knows his craft, but he can teach it to others so well that they can duplicate the process.

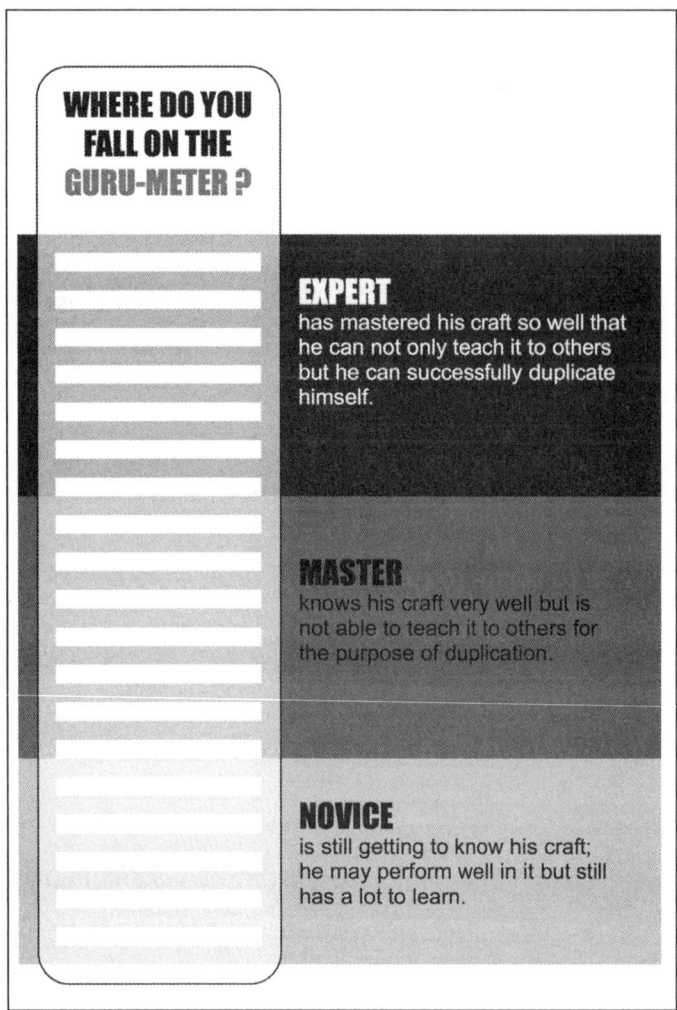

WHERE DO YOU FALL ON THE GURU-METER ?

EXPERT
has mastered his craft so well that he can not only teach it to others but he can successfully duplicate himself.

MASTER
knows his craft very well but is not able to teach it to others for the purpose of duplication.

NOVICE
is still getting to know his craft; he may perform well in it but still has a lot to learn.

Now, take a moment to write about the positive things you're working on to get you on the path to Greatness. Where did you fall on the Guru-Meter concerning those things?

What sources do you need to get next to or who do you need to talk to so you can get to the next level?

_____

_____

_____

_____

_____

_____

_____

_____

Repeat:

I'm good at what I do but I don't know everything.

Though you are searching for a mentor, think about who may look to you as a mentor. From what you have learned in GIUY, do you think you have the qualities consistent with that of a mentor?

_____

_____

_____

_____

_____

_____

_____

_____

How could you improve these skills. (Remember you don't know everything!)

_____

_____

_____

_____

_____

_____

_____

_____

_____

_____

LIVE IT

Admitting that you don't know it all is only the first step. Now, create a 7-day plan using the information from Day One to help you climb the Guru-Ladder.

Sunday _____

_____

_____

Monday _____

_____

_____

Tuesday _____

_____

_____

Wednesday _____

_____

_____

Thursday _____

_____

_____

Friday _____

_____

_____

Saturday _____

_____

_____

GREATNESS IS...

In my autobiography, The Secret to Success, I tell this story about a Guru and a young man who wanted to be successful. The young man seeks out the Guru to learn the mystery behind his success. Eager for the opportunity to get ahead, he meets the Guru at the beach, anxiously anticipating his lesson. The Guru, older, wiser, and unrestrained, looks the young man straight in his eyes and asks, "How bad do you want to be successful?" Giving it little to no thought, the young man answers, "Real bad." To his surprise, the Guru takes him by the hand and leads him out into the deep parts of the water.

When they were a little more than waist deep, the Guru grabs the young man, takes his head, and holds it down under the water. The young man, beating and slapping the water, fights to resist the Guru's attack; but he finds no relief until the Guru lets him up and asks him, "What was the one thing you wanted while you were under water?"

Gasping and wheezing for air, his heart racing partly from his struggle under water and partly from the uncertainty of what the Guru would do to him next, the young man stammers, "I wanted to breathe." Pleased, the Guru responded, "When you want to succeed as bad as you want to breathe, then you'll be successful."

Consider the things you have done to work towards your goals (i.e., classes you've taken, study time, overtime, investment of money, etc.). While his approach, to some, may seem unorthodox, the Guru was making a phenomenal point: we say we want success, we say we want to move to the next level... to step our game up, but most of us aren't willing to do what it will take to get there.

The biggest deterrent for many of us is our pride. We think we know more, we think we can do more, we think we're smarter, and more talented than the next guy. The thing that changed the young man's life wasn't just in the lesson he was taught, it was in the fact that he sought out the Guru to begin with. He needed to know something, and he was smart enough to know that he didn't have the answer, and so he searched for the person who did.

Greatness is acknowledging that as talented and successful as you may be, there is someone else who can show you more.

Spend time today reflecting on your actions this week.

Did you meet the challenge? If not, why?

_____

_____

_____

_____

_____

GREATNESS IS UPON YOU

CERTIFICATE OF COMPLETION

This is to certify that

_____

has successfully completed this week's challenge.

Eric Thomas and Associates, LLC

_____
signature

_____
date

WEEK 15
REPEL VS. ATTRACT
GREATNESS PRINCIPLE #15:
Greatness is not just seeking the information but acting on the body of knowledge you already have.

Finding the right mentor can be a long and tedious process. What if they're too busy or live too far away? How can you take advantage of the Mentor's wisdom if you can never talk to them? In the previous chapter we talked about the importance of seeking out help; this week, we discuss what you can do to bring your guru to you.

If you could have the mentor of your choice, who would it be? Why?

_____

_____

_____

_____

_____

_____

_____

_____

_____

_____

_____

_____

_____

_____

_____

_____

_____

_____

DAY ONE: LEARN IT

The question today is simple: What are you doing to attract your mentor? Are you inactively sitting and waiting for your guru to show up? Or are you living your dream and creating the opportunity that could change your life?

_____

_____

_____

_____

_____

DAY TWO: ACCEPT IT

Create a Mentor Wish List. Remember, this list is not about the characteristics you want in a mentor. This list is about the information you hope to gain from having a mentor.

_____

_____

_____

_____

_____

_____

_____

_____

In Chap. 14 you were asked to identify 3 people that you thought would be a great mentor.

What are you doing to attract your mentor? (What is your availability? What is your attitude? What are you doing in your spare time? Do you have goals in place?)

_____

_____

_____

_____

_____

_____

_____

DAY THREE: EMBRACE IT
Find out what makes the Greats in your field Great. Find out what schools they attended, what books they read, what hobbies they had, and model their behaviors.

_____

_____

_____

_____

_____

_____

_____

_____

Knowledge.

Take it a level higher, research 3 of the worlds most influential people.

Did they have help (i.e. mentor, supervisor)

_____

_____

_____

_____

_____

What were their biggest setbacks?

_____

_____

_____

_____

_____

How did they grow to become a success?

_____

_____

_____

_____

_____

_____

DAY FOUR: CHANGE IT

Get out and volunteer your time in your field of interest.

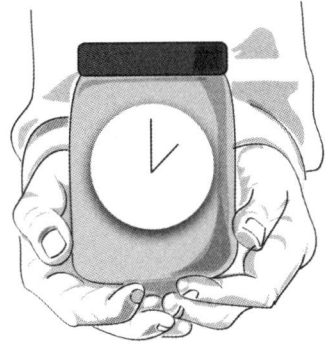 **VOLUNTEER YOUR TIME**

DAY FIVE: LIVE IT

What strategy can you create and implement to attract your guru to you?

Sunday _____

_____

_____

Monday _____

_____

_____

Tuesday _____

_____

_____

Wednesday _____

_____

_____

Thursday _____

_____

_____

Friday _____

_____

Saturday _____

GREATNESS IS...

"Phil Jackson. Phil Jackson is a – to me, he's a professional Dean Smith. He challenged me mentally, not just physically..."

[Excerpt from Michael Jordan's Basketball Hall of Fame Enshrinement Speech]

You've heard the story: Michael Jordan didn't make the Varsity team of his high school basketball team when he first started out. But he stayed in the game and continued to play anyway. He pursued his passion, gave 120% in every game and, in doing so, his efforts eventually made way for him to meet his mentor, Phil Jackson.

The rest is history.

Greatness is not just seeking the information but acting on the body of knowledge you already have.

Spend time today reflecting on your actions this week.

Did you meet the challenge? If not, why?

_____

_____

_____

_____

_____

_____

_____

_____

_____

GIUY RE-UP

In Summary, when it comes finding your mentor...

AVERAGE PEOPLE	GREATNESS...
Believe that they already know all that there is to know in their field.	*Requires a belief in one's own ignorance.*
Neglect their passion in search for a mentor.	*Requires commitment to your passion while understanding that there is someone out there who can help you get to the next level.*

Assess how well you've demonstrated your potential in this area on the scales below:

Before Reading :

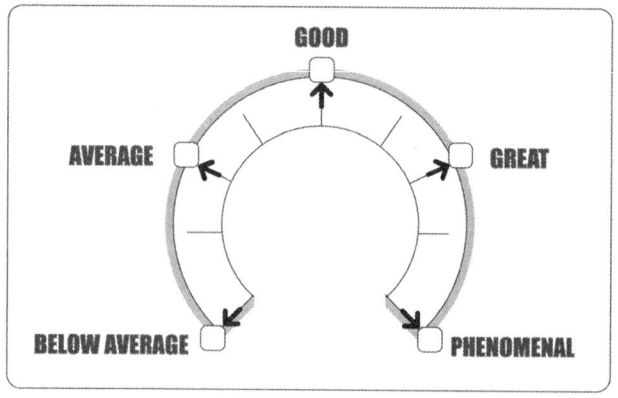

After Reading :

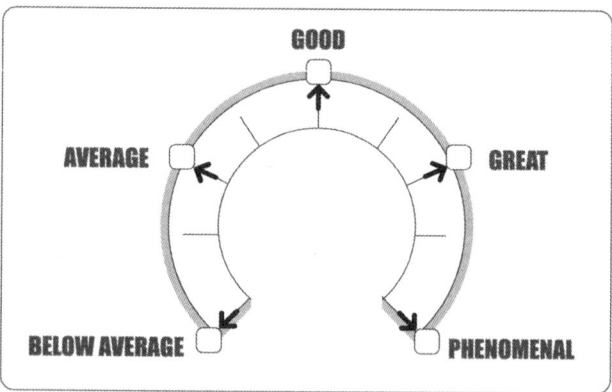

_____

_____

_____

_____

_____

_____

_____

_____

GREATNESS IS UPON YOU
CERTIFICATE OF COMPLETION

This is to certify that

_____

has successfully completed this week's challenge.

Eric Thomas and Associates, LLC

_____
signature

_____
date

WEEK 16
STAY VS. GO

GREATNESS PRINCIPLE #16:

Greatness is saying, "Yes, I am afraid of failing, but I'm more afraid of failing to try."

Does the thought of a new beginning scare you or excite you?

New beginnings are scary - I've had enough to know. Maybe you're thinking about going back to school, opening a new business, or starting a new relationship. You don't reach the top of the mountain from the top of the mountain. At some point, there was a bottom... there was a climb... there was a struggle and that first step up the mountain was the most important step because, without it, you'd still be at the bottom.

I once thought about ... _____

but decided not to because ... _____

_____

_____

_____

I would do ... _____

_____

but it takes a lot of ... _____

_____

_____

If I had ... _____

I would .... _____

_____

_____

_____

DAY ONE: LEARN IT

What mountain can you commit to climbing today?

_____

_____

_____

_____

_____

_____

_____

_____

_____

_____

_____

_____

_____

_____

_____

_____

_____

Create a realistic
TIMELINE

Create a realistic timeline that will identify the process from when you take your first step toward climbing your mountain to the day/event that will signify that you have made it to the top of your mountain. An example from my life would be a timeline showing the day that I filled out the application to take the GED course (my first step), and then every step leading up to me walking across the stage to accept my PhD (the top of my mountain).

What first step do you need to take?

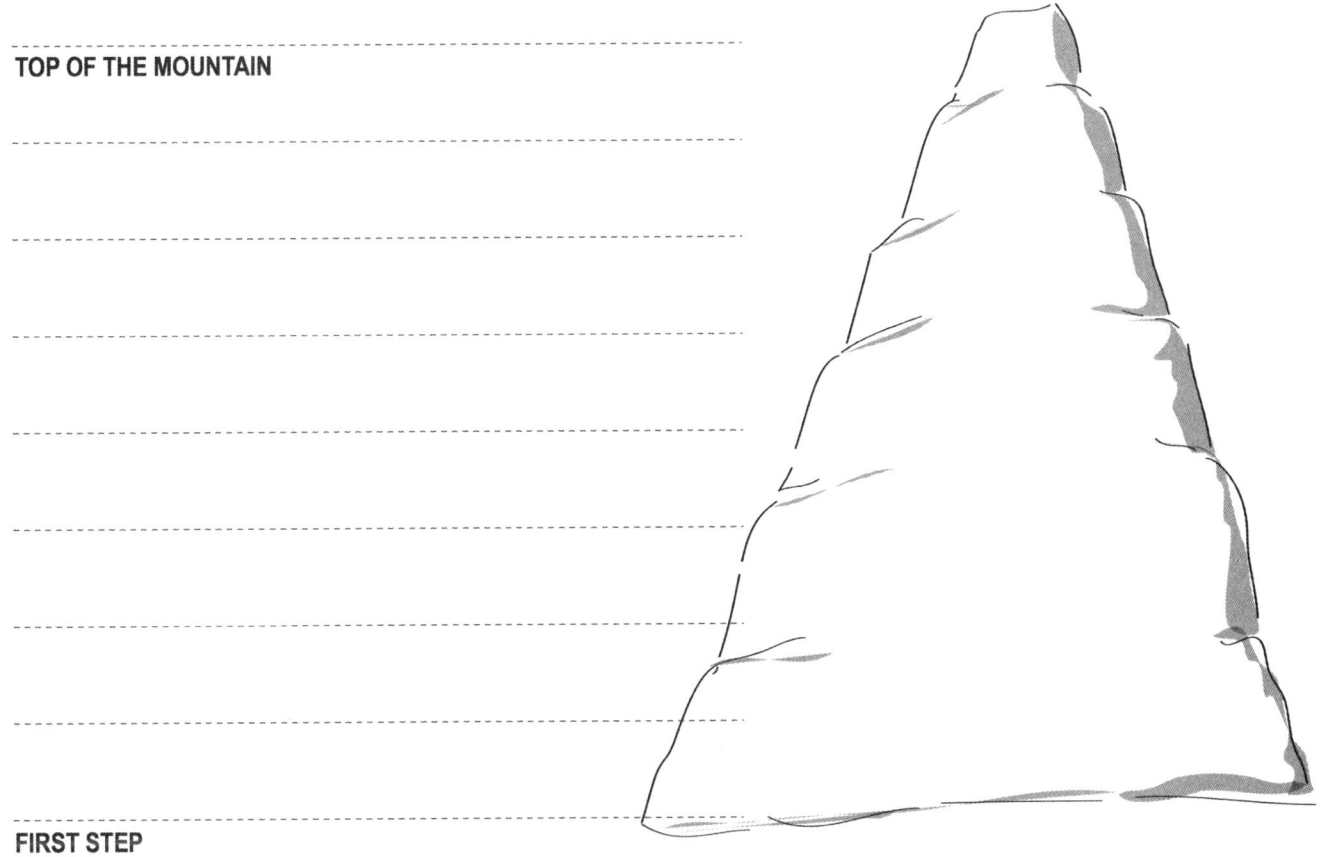

TOP OF THE MOUNTAIN

FIRST STEP

DAY TWO: ACCEPT IT

What is the one thing in your life that if you had no fears (i.e., no financial concerns, no ties, no restrictions, etc.) you would start on it right away?

_____

_____

_____

_____

_____

Write that challenge here:

I accept the fact that I haven't named my mountain. Today, I will take the first step and name my Mountain: _____

_____ *I promise myself that I will do*

_____

_____

_____

_____

and be _____

_____

_____

DAY THREE: EMBRACE IT

Whatever endeavor you've been wanting to start, begin the research on it today. What costs are associated with it?

_____

_____

_____

_____

What other people (in your life or in the media) have been successful at this endeavor?

_____

_____

_____

_____

How long does it take?

_____

_____

_____

_____

What is the process to get started?

_____

_____

_____

_____

DAY FOUR: CHANGE IT

1. Get rid of "Stinking Thinking."
2. Take ownership for your actions.
3. Take advantage of an opportunity of a lifetime in the lifetime of the opportunity.
4. Leave the Lurker's mindset behind.
5. Ask the guru.

You may know where you want to be, but not know how to get there. Below, use the sidewalk and the steps provided above to lay out the next 5 steps you need to take toward accomplishing your goal. Remember, these steps should be instrumental in helping you reach your goal.

Step 1	Step 2	Step 3	Step 4	Step 5

Now that you have some information to help you get started, how will you implement these ten steps to help you make that big change in your life?

_____

_____

_____

_____

_____

_____

_____

_____

What additional things can you do to help you start your new endeavor?

_____

_____

_____

_____

_____

_____

_____

_____

DAY FIVE: LIVE IT

Today, you set your climb in action by taking the 1st step. In your research on Day Three, you were asked to learn the necessary process for achieving your goal. For instance, if your mountain involves going to school or joining the service, you might have learned in your research that there is an application process. If this is the case, print and fill out the application today. The very first step you take should be the first step you listed on your timeline. Create your 7-day plan to make your new beginning.

Sunday _____

_____

_____

Monday _____

_____

_____

Tuesday _____

_____

_____

Wednesday _____

_____

Thursday _____

_____

_____

Friday _____

_____

_____

Saturday _____

_____

_____

GREATNESS IS...

Innovation.

Love them or hate them, everyone knows the name Ford. Henry Ford didn't invent the automobile. He wasn't even responsible for the first assembly line, but what he did to change the game was that he was brave enough to step out and take chance after chance after chance at something he had never done before and he took it and revolutionized the industry. He was fired from his first job and his first two companies were failures, but he kept moving in the direction of his mountain.

Listen, sometimes that first step you take might set you back two or three more steps, but you've got to make up in your mind that you're ok with the consequences. Something inside of you has to value the process more than the temporary upsets.

There are a million motivational speakers and coaches in this industry, the odds were against me before I even delivered my first speech, but I knew that if I could just keep my eyes on the peak of the mountain... though the winds were rising steadily against me and a thousand obstacles stood in my way, I was anchored... steadfast... unmovable... unshakeable... I knew that there was something for me if I just allowed myself to move with the currents.

And the reason that many people will never see the top of their mountains, is because they become so paralyzed by the fear of not making it past the first step.

Greatness is saying, "Yes, I am afraid of failing, but I'm more afraid of failing to try."

Spend time today reflecting on your actions this week.

Did you meet the challenge? If not, why?

_____

GREATNESS IS UPON YOU
CERTIFICATE OF COMPLETION

This is to certify that

_____

has successfully completed this week's challenge.

Eric Thomas and Associates, LLC

_____
signature

_____
date

WEEK 17
EXTINGUISHING THE FIRE VS. FUELING THE FIRE

Are you fueling your flames or letting them die out?

It's frustrating for many people to set goals for themselves and then look back on them years later just to find their goals incomplete. What is the common denominator to our unsuccessful endeavors? This week we investigate how factors external to your goal affect your ability to achieve desired outcomes.

What is the ONE goal you've set for yourself that you haven't been able to accomplish up to this day?

_____

_____

_____

_____

_____

_____

_____

_____

_____

_____

_____

_____

_____

_____

DAY ONE: LEARN IT

What Extinguishing Fire factors are prevalent in your life? List them below.

_____

_____

_____

_____

_____

_____

DAY TWO: ACCEPT IT

List 3 areas in your life where you need to fortify your environment because the fire is missing. i.e., My relationship with my parents.

1. _____

_____

2. _____

_____

3. _____

_____

Take one of the areas that you identified and think of 3-5 things that you can do to reignite that fire!

1. _____
_____

2. _____
_____

3. _____
_____

4. _____
_____

5. _____
_____

DAY THREE: EMBRACE IT

Describe what "Fueling your fire" skills your friends possess and how you specifically plan to call on these skills. Identify what times in your life you will need to call on them.

_____
_____
_____
_____
_____
_____
_____
_____
_____
_____
_____
_____

Your passion to complete a personal task is the driving force on whether it happens or not. Pick three current scenario's in your life, identifying the heat and fuel. Pay close attention to the oxygen, your environment plays a huge role in your success as well.

	Heat
HEAT Initial ignition of fire FUEL OXYGEN Combustible Support Material	
	Fuel
	Oxygen

HEAT
Initial
ignition
of fire

FUEL
Combustible
Material

FIRE

OXYGEN
Support

Heat

Fuel

Oxygen

HEAT
Initial
ignition
of fire

FUEL
Combustible
Material

FIRE

OXYGEN
Support

Heat

Fuel

Oxygen

Being prepared for life's unpredictable moments takes work. Use this space to predict the possible issues that may affect your current scenarios above. This will help you to have solutions or different routes in place, not interrupting your original goals.

_____

_____

_____

_____

_____

_____

DAY FOUR: CHANGE IT

Protecting your environment is essential to your cause.

Protect : What can you do to build a more stable environment for the goal(s) that you've set?

_____

_____

_____

_____

_____

_____

Forecast: What are the potential threats?

_____

_____

_____

_____

_____

_____

DAY FIVE: LIVE IT

Don't get caught off guard - stay ahead of the game. Create a 7-day plan for how you will make the needed adjustments to your environment to help you stay consistent.

Sunday _____

_____

_____

Monday _____

_____

_____

Tuesday _____

_____

_____

Wednesday _____

_____

_____

Thursday _____

_____

_____

Friday _____

_____

_____

Saturday _____

_____

_____

GREATNESS IS...

Remember the story of the Rabbit and the Turtle?

The Rabbit was bragging about how fast he was, and the Turtle challenges him to a race. Everything about the Rabbit said that he should have won this race, he was stronger and faster and, let's face it, he was going up against a turtle! Why wouldn't he win? Yet, he didn't. And this was a great disappointment; but the only thing that cost him the race - was him.

The thing that destroyed the Rabbit's success wasn't his confidence in his abilities, it wasn't his intellect, and it wasn't that the turtle had some super natural gift. The goal had been set, he had the desire to win, and everyone in his environment believed that he would do it, but then he decided to stop and take a nap. He sabotaged his own success by killing his fire, because even though it was only for a few minutes, he no longer desired to keep running. And those minutes cost him everything.

Think about what one day of not working out does to your weight loss goal; what one day of not doing your homework does to your goal of getting your diploma or degree. What does one day of not writing a page in your book do to your momentum?

The Rabbit killed his own momentum by stopping - he wasn't consistent.

Consistency is the powerhouse of every successful endeavor. I'm not saying it's easy, but it is necessary if you want to see yourself move to the next level.

Greatness is resisting the temptation to throw in the towel even when everything in your environment says you should.

Spend time today reflecting on your actions this week.

Did you meet the challenge? If not, why?

_____

_____

_____

_____

_____

_____

_____

_____

_____

GREATNESS IS UPON YOU

CERTIFICATE OF COMPLETION

This is to certify that

_____

has successfully completed this week's challenge.

Eric Thomas and Associates, LLC

_____
signature

_____
date

WEEK 18
LOST IN GRIEF VS. WORKING THROUGH PAIN

GREATNESS PRINCIPLE #18:
Greatness is remembering in the dark what God told you in the light.

Do you allow yourself to get lost in grief or do you find a way to push through it?

Right now, you may be experiencing some hardships (or the aftermath of some hardships). Perhaps you're recently divorced, or lost a loved one... or maybe you feel like everything you touch is a failure, and you don't know which way to go. Just remember that the darkest moment in the night is when the sun begins to rise.

Moment of Silence.

DAY ONE: LEARN IT

It's not easy, but it's necessary. write about a moment in your life that made it necessary for you to push past the pain.

MOVE PAST THE PAIN

CHANGE IT

EMBRACE IT

ACCEPT IT

LEARN IT

_____

_____

_____

_____

_____

_____

DAY TWO: ACCEPT IT

Certain situations can be hard to talk about and handle on your own. Use this space to look up poems or songs that may help you handle your difficult situations.

_____

_____

_____

_____

_____

_____

_____

_____

_____

_____

_____

EXPRESS YOUR FEELING ABOUT YOUR HARDSHIPS
CREATIVELY
by writing a poem, lyrics to a song, a painting, etc.

Use how your feel-ing, and write your own poem or song.

DAY THREE: EMBRACE IT

HELP SOMEONE THAT YOU KNOW WHO IS GOING THROUGH HARDSHIPS

What can you do for a family member, friend, or colleague today?

DAY FOUR: CHANGE IT

COMMIT TO A NEW
NEW WORKOUT
enjoy the energetic rush!

Commit to a new workout activity today. Run an extra mile, try the elliptical instead of the treadmill, take a spin class, join a Zumba class, or simply change sceneries and walk at a different park. Whatever you do, make it active, and allow yourself to burn away the sadness and enjoy the energetic rush!

As you are working out, think through what new meaningful experience can be created through your loss. Identify it here:

_____

_____

_____

_____

_____

_____

_____

_____

DAY FIVE: LIVE IT

The goal is to find the Beauty in your Loss. Create a 7-day plan that you can commit to to help you begin the move past your pain.

Sunday _____

_____

_____

Monday _____

_____

_____

Tuesday _____

_____

_____

Wednesday _____

_____

_____

Thursday _____

_____

Friday _____

_____

_____

Saturday _____

_____

_____

GREATNESS IS...

Imagine waking up to what seems like a normal day. You get up and open your blinds to see the sunrise from your bedroom patio and there isn't a cloud in the sky. You reach for your morning cup of coffee when suddenly the phone rings; it's your broker calling to tell you that the market crashed, and you've lost all of your assets. You're arguing with your broker about how this could possibly happen considering the flawless portfolio he showed you yesterday. As he begins to move into an explanation, your other line begins to <<beep>>. You click over to hear your lawyer tell you that the property you just closed on was illegally obtained, and not only did you have to stop all plans to break ground for the new shopping mall, you just hired dozens of contractors to build; but the guy who sold you the property is nowhere to be found. Practically numb from what could only be described as the trailer to the movie, The Worst Day Ever, you get a knock at the door and, eager for even the slightest bit of relief, you run down the stairs to answer the door and find a police officer standing in your doorway. Confused, you ask him to come in. He enters apologizing, explaining to you that your family was the fourth car in a twenty car pile up on the Interstate and, unfortunately, there were no survivors.

Extreme? Maybe. But my point is that devastation can strike at any moment.

The reason I love the story of Job so much is because it exemplifies for me the mentality we all should have when we've suffered a loss. Job had everything. And without warning, it was all gone. He lost his riches, his children were murdered, he became severely ill, and his wife lost faith in his beliefs. Through his anguish, depression, and heartache, he never denied the one thing that sustained him. He said, "The Lord giveth and the Lord taketh away. Blessed be the name of the Lord." I've lost everyone and everything that ever mattered to me but, "Blessed be the name of the Lord." I've worked hard and done everything I was supposed to do but, "Blessed be the name of the Lord." My friends don't understand me but, "Blessed be the name of the Lord." My wife has turned her back on me but, "Blessed be the name of the Lord." My enemies rejoice in their iniquities while I have lived a pure and righteous life but, "Blessed be the name of the Lord." I feel broken, defeated, and full of despair but, "Blessed be the name of the Lord."

Greatness is making a decision. Greatness is deciding that darkness is darkness, but darkness will not destroy you. Greatness is not letting your agony consume you and getting through it all with your integrity intact.

Many of us have been devastated by sudden or even anticipated tragedies. But you have to learn to go through pain (in whatever form it is presented to you) without allowing it to break your spirit. No one gets excited about the dark moments when they hit, but the Greats use tragedies to their advantage. Even in the midst of catastrophic adversity, Job didn't succumb to the pressure that his wounds had stacked against him, he was beaten but he didn't break.

Greatness is remembering in the dark what God told you in the light.

Spend time today reflecting on your actions this week.

Did you meet the challenge? If not, why?

_____

_____

_____

_____

_____

_____

_____

_____

_____

_____

_____

_____

_____

_____

_____

_____

_____

_____

GREATNESS IS UPON YOU

GREATNESS IS UPON YOU

CERTIFICATE OF COMPLETION

This is to certify that

_____

has successfully completed this week's challenge.

Eric Thomas and Associates, LLC

_____
signature

_____
date

WEEK 19
"SOMETIMES", "MAYBE", "I'M NOT SURE" VS. 120% "ALL IN"

GREATNESS PRINCIPLE #19:
Greatness is the end result of consistency backed by an unbreachable promise.

Are you tapped out at 80% or are you "ALL IN"?

In chapter 18, we talked about why it's important to be consistent Lets take it a step further and explore not just the need to be consistent but to consistently give 120% in everything that we do.

I consistently put 120% into:

☐ My Career   ☐ My Family   ☐ My Goals

☐ My Dreams   ☐ My School Work   ☐ My Other Commitments

_____

_____

_____

_____

_____

_____

_____

_____

_____

_____

_____

_____

_____

_____

LEARN IT

What challenges or obstacles do you face that actively inhibit your ability to go ALL IN? In these areas of your life, have you proven yourself to be one who gets discouraged and quits (under contract), or have you proven yourself to be one who picks up the pieces and recreates destiny (lives by covenant)?

_____

_____

_____

_____

_____

_____

_____

_____

_____

_____

BEING UNDER
CONTRACT

VS

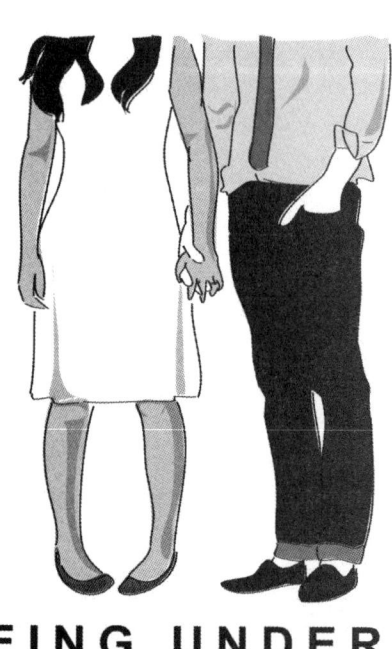

BEING UNDER
COVENANT

What contracts are you in, that you would rather make a covenant? (i.e. your relationships, your faith, your character.)

_____

_____

_____

_____

_____

_____

_____

_____

ACCEPT IT

CONTRACT

I accept the fact that I am not consistent in bringing my "A" game everyday.

_____

_____

_____

_____

_____

EMBRACE IT

I vow to give 120% to be All In in spite of the fact that

_____

_____

even when my haters

_____

_____

and when the circumstances are not quite

_____

_____

CHANGE IT

Let's identify all of the times that you don't go ALL IN (bring your "A" game), and then identify the patterns you notice in each situation. What personal reasons do you have for not showing up consistently and giving your all in every aspect. (i.e., lack passion, little to no direction, complacency, etc.)?

_____

_____

_____

_____

_____

_____

_____

_____

If you didn't make the changes in this area of your life, who would you be letting down and why?

_____

_____

_____

_____

_____

_____

_____

_____

LIVE IT

We've already discussed how consistency is a key factor in your ability to be successful. What can you do to make sure that you consistently bring your "A" game to every endeavor? Develop your 7-day plan to get the most out of yourself.

Sunday _____

_____

Monday _____

_____

Tuesday _____

_____

Wednesday _____

_____

Thursday _____

_____

Friday _____

_____

_____

Saturday _____

_____

_____

GREATNESS IS...

There's a popular illustration of two men digging for diamonds. In the illustration, the guy on the top is hammering away to get to the diamonds, but you can tell that he still has a ways to go. Meanwhile, the guy on the bottom, has stopped hammering and is walking in the opposite direction of the diamonds and, from the illustration, you can tell that if he had just given the gravel one or two more whacks with his hammer, the diamonds would have all come rushing out.

I've seen people use this illustration as an example of why we should never give up. But what if the guy at the bottom didn't intend to give up and was simply tired from all of the hammering he had been doing? So instead of hammering away at full speed, he decided to relax and take a break? The results are still the same. Whether you give up completely or you decide to just give 60% effort one day out of 7 days, you risk missing out on collecting diamonds. Is this a risk you're willing to take?

Consistency is not your burden. Actually, it is the one thing that can effectively alleviate any burdens you may have.

In Biblical times, covenants were considered sacred, because it signified a promise that would never be broken. There are certain disappointments that will prove to be inevitable simply because we're expecting a covenant relationship but putting in contract effort.

> ***Greatness is the end result of consistency backed by an unbreachable promise.***

Spend time today reflecting on your actions this week.

Did you meet the challenge? If not, why?

_____

_____

_____

GIUY RE-UP

AVERAGE PEOPLE	GREATNESS...
Allow fear to keep them from reaching their goals.	*Requires the courage to get up and GO!*
Don't plan for changes in their environment.	*Requires forecasting to keep the fire burning.*
Allow themselves to be consumed by their pain.	*Requires using your pain to help you move forward.*
Allow setbacks to keep them from moving forward.	*Requires a knack for creating opportunities out of setbacks.*

Assess how well you've demonstrated your potential in this area on the scales below:

Before Reading :   **After Reading :**

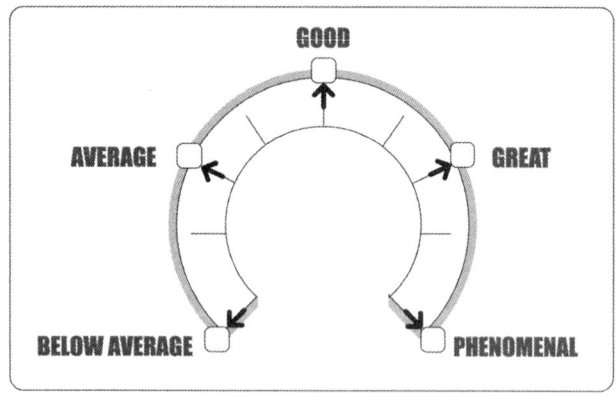 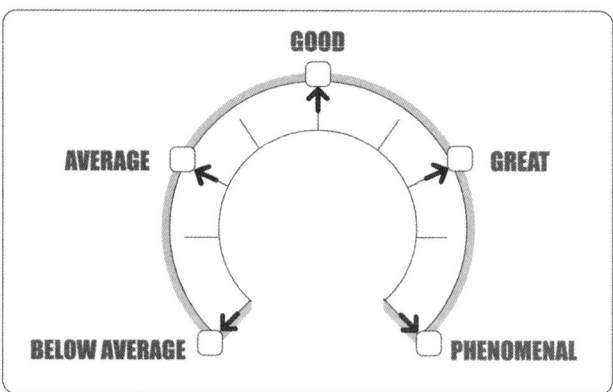

_____

_____

_____

_____

_____

_____

_____

_____

GREATNESS IS UPON YOU
CERTIFICATE OF COMPLETION

This is to certify that

_____

has successfully completed this week's challenge.

Eric Thomas and Associates, LLC

_____
signature

_____
date

WEEK 20
BEATEN VS. BESTED

GREATNESS PRINCIPLE #20:
Greatness is refusing to allow yourself to get beat out of the opportunity to fully realize your potential.

Are setbacks merely setbacks for you or an opportunity for a comeback?

You might be thinking, "My boss is crazy; my wife isn't acting right; my kids are out of control; my money isn't right; etc." But none of these things matter when you consider the Big picture. Look at the negative and turn it around - you only get one life, one opportunity, ONE shot!

There's a lot of material about how to cope with pain or how to handle setbacks. What sources do you trust when you're going through your more difficult moments?

_____

_____

_____

_____

_____

_____

_____

_____

_____

_____

_____

_____

_____

_____

_____

DAY ONE: LEARN IT

In general, how do you handle major upsets or disappointments? Who do you talk to? What are your behaviors?

_____

_____

_____

_____

_____

_____

_____

DAY TWO: ACCEPT IT

THINK ABOUT "LEMONS" LIFE HAS THROWN YOU

Think about some of the "lemons" that life has thrown you (i.e., fatherless home, death of a parent/child, laid off from your job, failed company, etc.).

How did you handle this situation?

_____

_____

_____

_____

_____

_____

_____

What outlets did you use to push you forward?

_____

_____

_____

_____

_____

_____

Who were the key people involved in helping you move ahead?

_____

_____

_____

_____

_____

_____

Who were the key people involved in keeping you behind?

_____

_____

_____

_____

_____

_____

_____

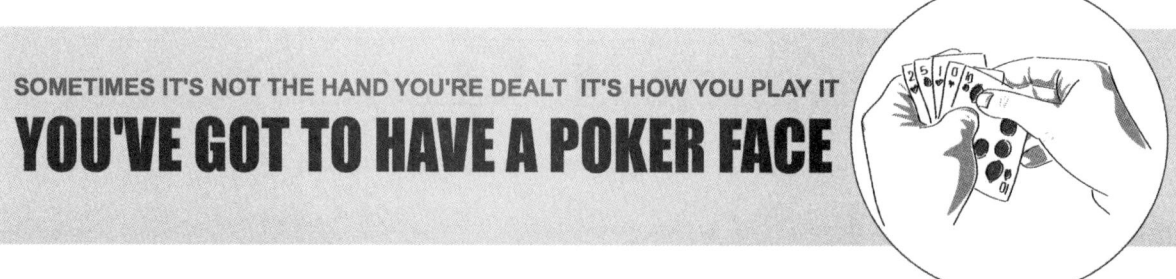

SOMETIMES IT'S NOT THE HAND YOU'RE DEALT IT'S HOW YOU PLAY IT

YOU'VE GOT TO HAVE A POKER FACE

DAY THREE: EMBRACE IT

Below are 4 cards with 4 different "lemon" scenarios. Underneath each card, write what your initial reaction to the situation would be and then describe a reaction that would allow you to move on with your day in a more healthy way (i.e., make lemonade).

1	2	3	4
You're on your way to work and you get cut off in traffic. This followed by an unpleasant hand gesture.	You sat up all night working on a report for school/work and your teacher/boss barely looks at it after you turn it in.	You get a phone call from your child's principal saying they have been suspended from school.	You find out that you didn't get the job that you interviewed for.

GENUINE REACTION	GENUINE REACTION	GENUINE REACTION	GENUINE REACTION

BETTER REACTION	BETTER REACTION	BETTER REACTION	BETTER REACTION

DAY FOUR: CHANGE IT

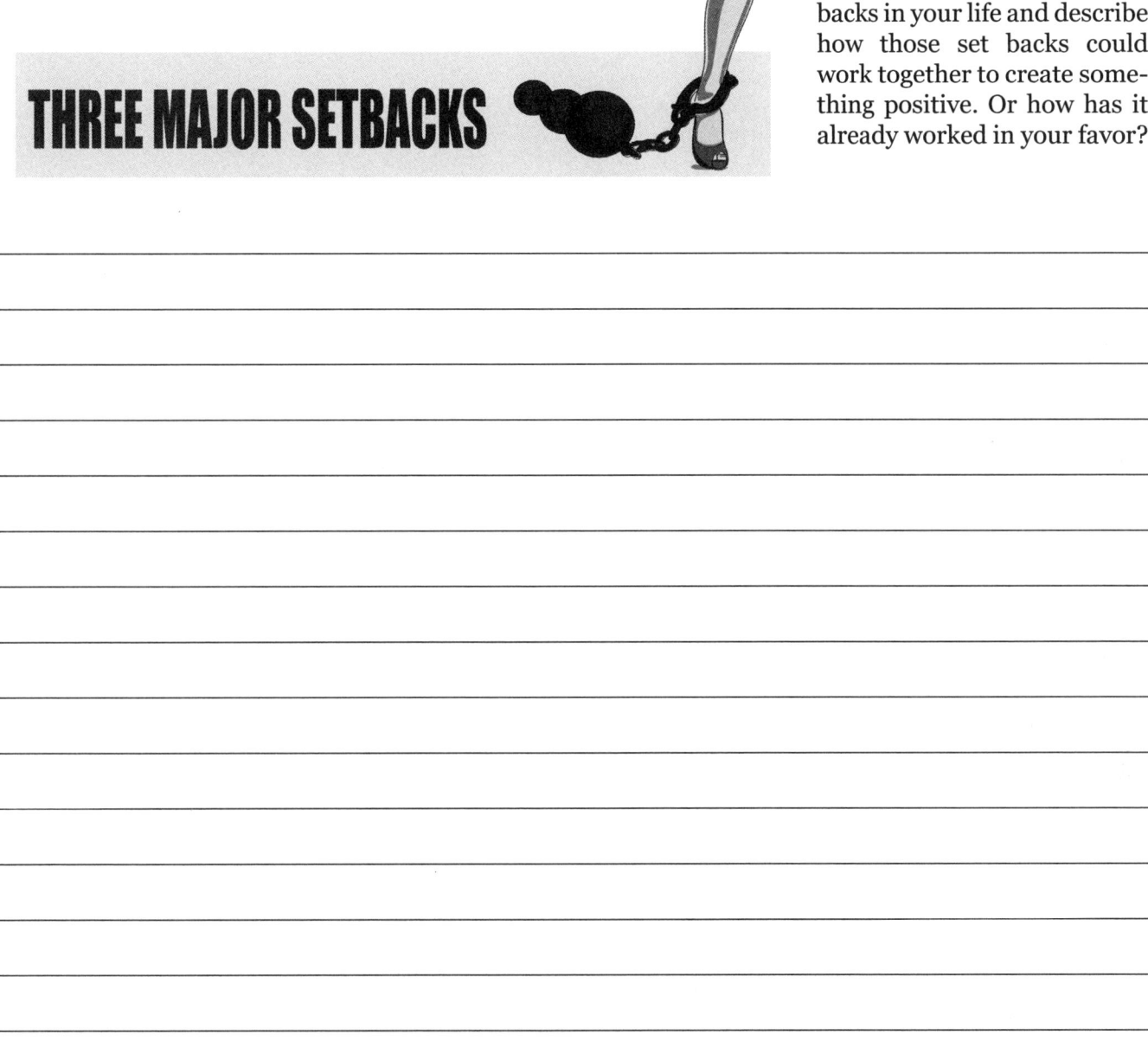

Think about three major set backs in your life and describe how those set backs could work together to create something positive. Or how has it already worked in your favor?

_____

_____

_____

_____

_____

_____

_____

_____

_____

_____

_____

_____

_____

_____

_____

_____

_____

_____

_____

_____

_____

Maybe you've already mastered perseverance and making the most out of unfavorable circumstances. But if you haven't, what changes would you need to make to become a person who makes the best out of a bad day, week, month, or year? The steps below helped me to make my transition

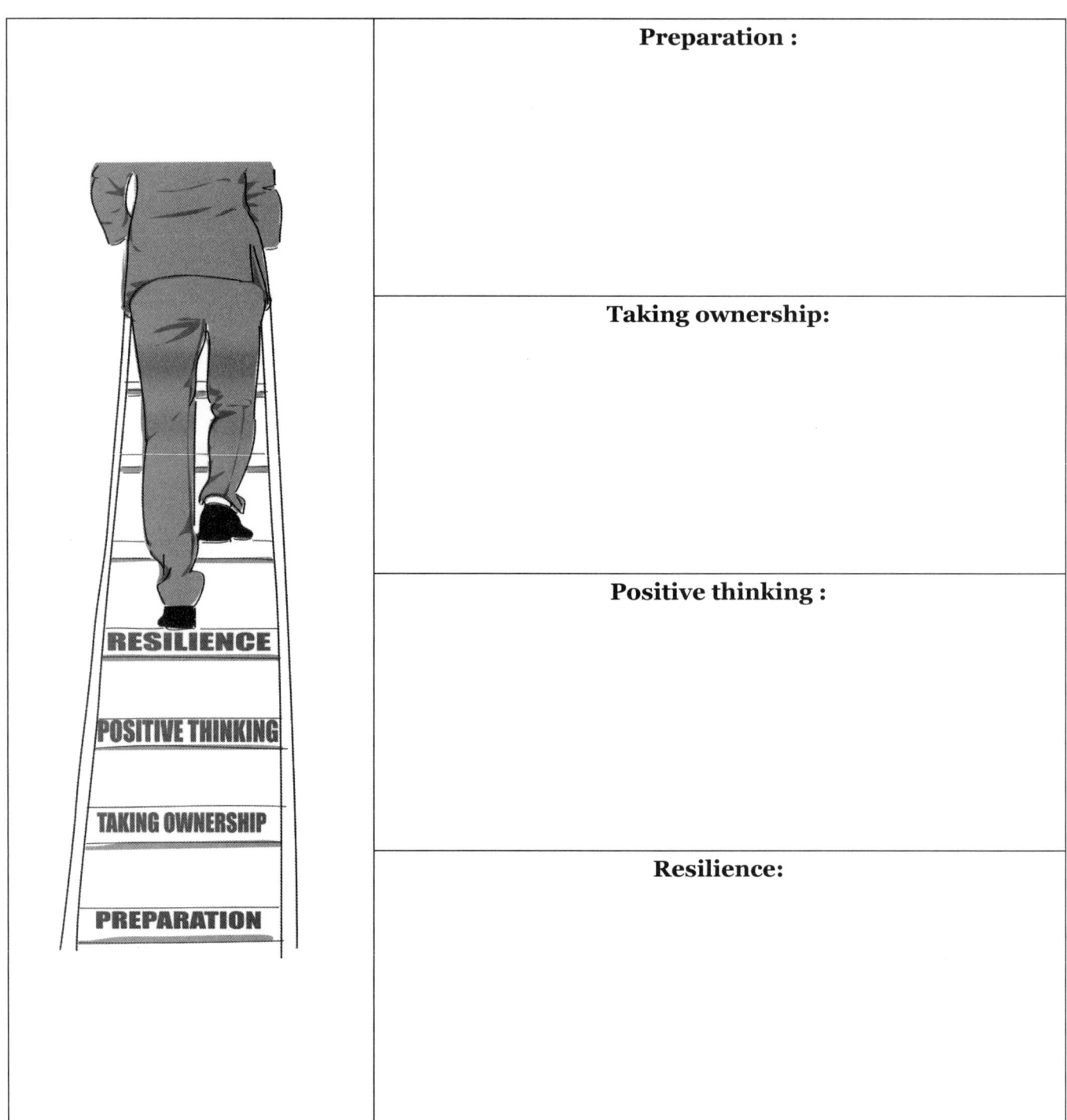

Preparation :

Taking ownership:

Positive thinking :

Resilience:

DAY FIVE: LIVE IT

What do you need to do to make sure that you're not allowing yourself to get caught up by the obstacles that life throws in your path? How will you personally be able to find the pleasure or make the most out of unfortunate situations? Create your 7-day plan for this area and commit to using it next week.

Sunday _____

_____

_____

Monday _____

_____

_____

Tuesday _____

_____

_____

Wednesday _____

_____

_____

Thursday _____

_____

_____

Friday _____

_____

_____

Saturday _____

_____

_____

GREATNESS IS...

I did some research on Adele a while back and discovered that when she was trying to record the album, 21, that she would spend hours in the studio but, eventually, she had to stop the project for months because the creativity wasn't at the level that it needed to be. But then her man, at the time, broke up with her. And not only did he break up with her, he got with someone else and was engaged in a matter of weeks.

She was talented. She was gifted. She already had her share of successes but after that breakup, she thought that her world had ended; but she didn't just sit in the pain and let it consume her. She was broken, but she didn't let herself stay there. She would have been justified in doing any number of things considering the circumstances, but instead, she got up and went back to the studio and belted out a record breaking album, earning seven Grammys, two Brit awards, twelve Billboard awards, and the list goes on.

In one move, she altered the course of her whole life out of the pain of the thing that she thought would destroy her.

Greatness is refusing to allow yourself to get beat out of the opportunity to fully realize your potential.

Spend time today reflecting on your actions this week.

Did you meet the challenge? If not, why?

_____

_____

_____

_____

_____

_____

_____

_____

_____

_____

_____

GREATNESS IS UPON YOU

CERTIFICATE OF COMPLETION

This is to certify that

_____

has successfully completed this week's challenge.

Eric Thomas and Associates, LLC

_____

signature

_____

date

WEEK 21
DESERT VS. VISION

GREATNESS PRINCIPLE #21:

Greatness is not just about making the best out of whatever life gives you, it's also about commitment to your vision at all costs.

When you're looking at a desert, do you see mounds of endless sand or endless opportunities?

When life knocks you down, it's a necessity to know who you are, what you want out of life, and why you want it. In short, nothing should be able to make you break your commitment to your vision. You may have to make adjustments depending on the "lemons" that come your way, but you still must move on with the vision in mind.

Complete the statements below:

*Vision is*_____

_____

_____

_____

_____

Vision requires _____

_____

_____

_____

_____

*I am distracted from my vision when*_____

_____

_____

_____

_____

DAY ONE: LEARN IT

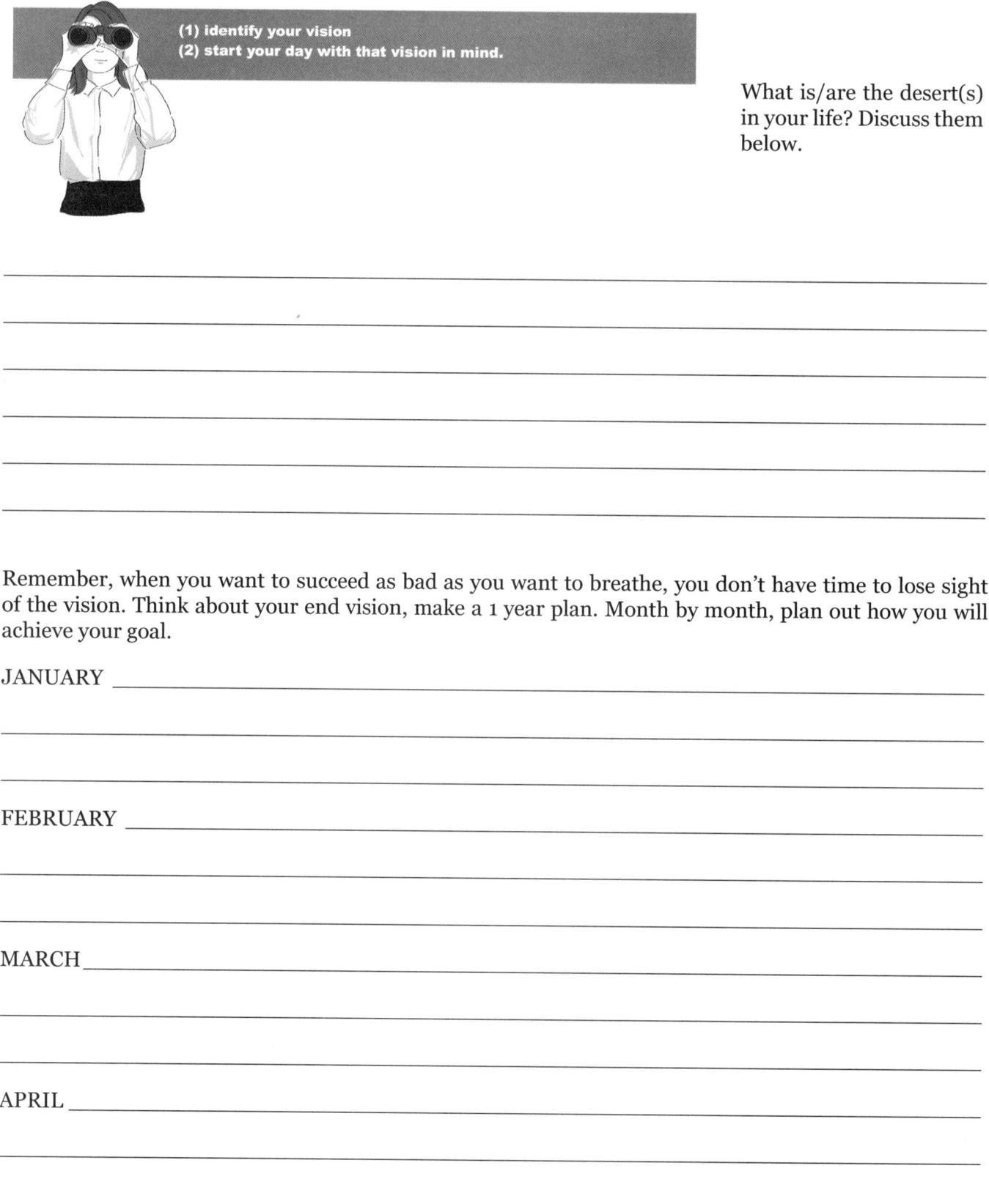

(1) identify your vision
(2) start your day with that vision in mind.

What is/are the desert(s) in your life? Discuss them below.

_____

_____

_____

_____

_____

_____

Remember, when you want to succeed as bad as you want to breathe, you don't have time to lose sight of the vision. Think about your end vision, make a 1 year plan. Month by month, plan out how you will achieve your goal.

JANUARY _____

_____

_____

FEBRUARY _____

_____

_____

MARCH_____

_____

_____

APRIL_____

_____

_____

MAY

JUNE

JULY

AUGUST

SEPTEMBER

OCTOBER

NOVEMBER

DECEMBER

DAY TWO: ACCEPT IT

Write your Morning Statement below. Rewrite it and put it somewhere you can see it every morning.

Original Morning Statement:_____

_____

_____

_____

_____

_____

_____

_____

Adapted Morning Statement: _____

_____

_____

_____

_____

_____

_____

_____

Adapted Morning Statement: _____

_____

_____

_____

_____

_____

_____

_____

Adapted Morning Statement: _____

_____

_____

_____

_____

_____

_____

_____

DAY THREE: EMBRACE IT

WHAT WOULD YOU WANT TO BE INCLUDED IN YOUR EULOGY?

If you were to die today, what would you want to be included in your eulogy? What type of lifestyle do you want to be remembered for living? Who do you hope to have impacted?

_____

_____

DAY FOUR: CHANGE IT

Today, create a list of your own Principles to live by.

_____

_____

_____

_____

_____

_____

_____

_____

_____

_____

_____

_____

_____

_____

_____

_____

_____

_____

_____

_____

_____

_____

_____

_____

DAY FIVE: LIVE IT

Remember, you can use your pain to push you to greatness but you'll need a vision. Create your 7-day plan of how you will work to define your vision or steps you will take to make your vision a reality.

Sunday _____

_____

_____

Monday _____

_____

_____

Tuesday _____

_____

_____

Wednesday _____

_____

_____

Thursday _____

_____

_____

Friday _____

_____

_____

Saturday _____

_____

_____

GREATNESS IS...

In the Bible, there is a story about a man named Jacob who met a woman, who would shortly thereafter, become the love of his life, Rachel. Desperately in love, he went to her father and told him that he would work seven years to have her hand in marriage. Rachel's father agreed that he would rather Rachel marry Jacob than anyone else, and so Jacob began to work. These seven years felt like nothing to Jacob, because he was so in love and so focused on the end goal.

When the seven years were complete, he went to Rachel's father for her hand in marriage. There was a huge wedding, and they became husband and wife... or so Jacob thought. As it turned out, the woman that he married was Leah, Rachel's older sister. When Jacob confronted Rachel's dad about the deception, he explained that it was against their custom to allow the youngest daughter to get married before the eldest. Rachel's father promised Jacob that, if he worked another seven years, he would give him Rachel's hand in marriage. Jacob worked those additional seven years with as much passion and fervor as he did the first seven because in spite of the fact that he was tricked and set back from his original plans, his vision was to marry Rachel, and he was willing to do whatever he needed to do to be with her.

What am I saying? Listen, sometimes things don't work out the way we planned. We can do everything right - dot every "i", cross every "t," but somehow someone or something (some trauma or event) interrupts the flow. Jacob would have had every right to be pissed. He could have walked away with Leah and never returned, he could have left Leah behind altogether and just abort his whole plan, or any number of other things. But instead he chose to make the adjustment with his vision in mind, and he worked the additional seven years to get what he wanted. For fourteen years Jacob got up everyday thinking, "I'm going to marry Rachel." Life without her was his desert, but he knew what he needed to do to change it.

Greatness is not just about making the best out of whatever life gives you, it's also about commitment to your vision at all costs.

Spend time today reflecting on your actions this week.

Did you meet the challenge? If not, why?

_____

_____

_____

_____

_____

_____

_____

_____

GREATNESS IS UPON YOU

CERTIFICATE OF COMPLETION

This is to certify that

_____

has successfully completed this week's challenge.

Eric Thomas and Associates, LLC

_____
signature

_____
date

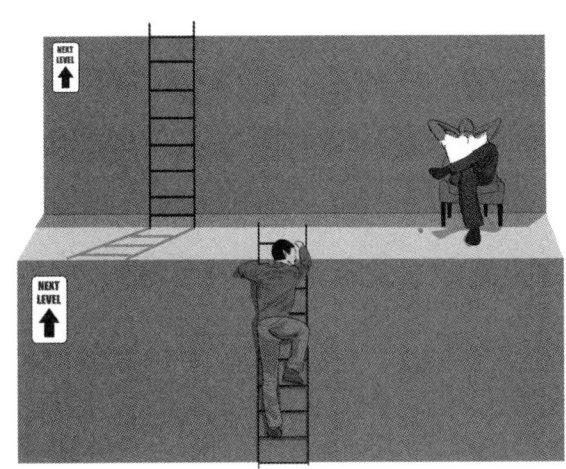

WEEK 22
PERFORM VS. OUTPERFORM
GREATNESS PRINCIPLE #22:
Greatness is expanding your portfolio to create more opportunities to stretch yourself.

Are you content with the success you've acquired at this point or are you ready for the next challenge?

You can perform and stay in the pocket, or you can push yourself to the next level and set the standard there as well. In this chapter we look at different performance levels and discuss why it's important to move out of the pocket.

Are you satisfied with your current level of success?

_____

_____

_____

_____

_____

_____

_____

_____

_____

_____

_____

_____

_____

_____

_____

_____

_____

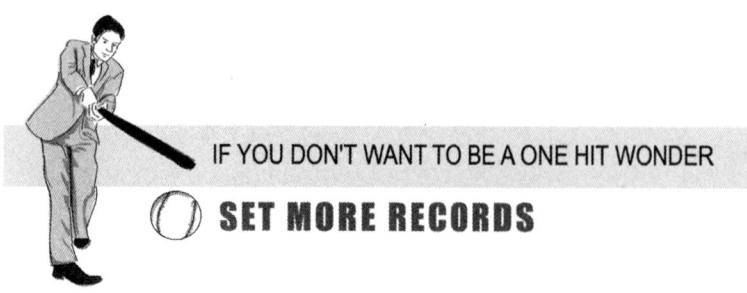

IF YOU DON'T WANT TO BE A ONE HIT WONDER

SET MORE RECORDS

If you don't want to be a one hit wonder, you have to keep grinding. You can't trophy watch and get so caught up in your accomplishments that you're looking at the score board instead of playing the game. You cannot settle.

DAY ONE: LEARN IT

Repeat this statement:

I am where I am today because of what I did yesterday. But what I did yesterday is not going to help me tomorrow.

What is your latest success?

_____

_____

_____

_____

_____

_____

_____

_____

_____

_____

_____

_____

_____

_____

_____

_____

_____

DAY TWO: ACCEPT IT

Shade in your level of performance in each of the areas above. Be honest with yourself. You will see that ou might be a Peak performer in one area and only a level performer in other areas.

_____

_____

_____

_____

_____

_____

_____

_____

_____

_____

DAY THREE: EMBRACE IT

Find one person who you trust from each of the areas in Day Two and ask them to rate what level of performance they think you are on in the area that is relevant to them.

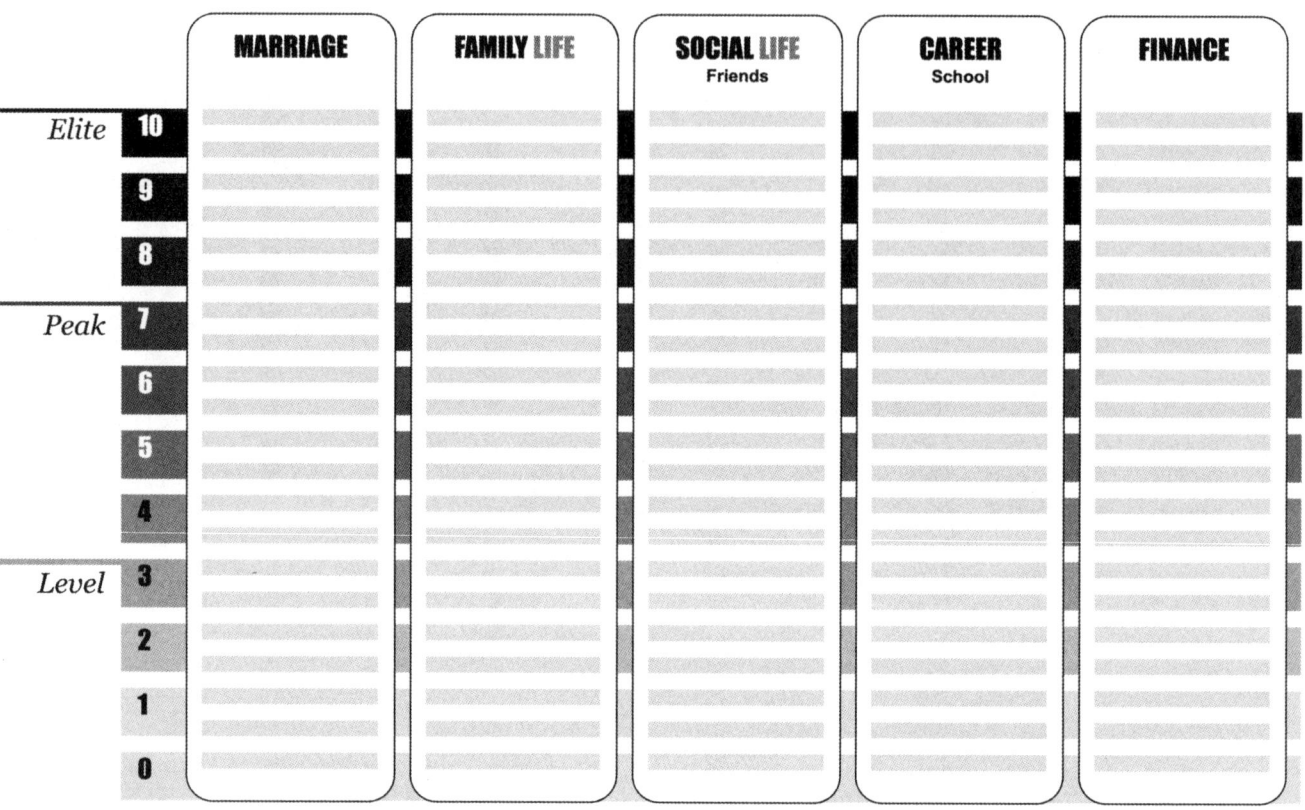

What are the consistencies when you compare it to what you recorded in Day Two? What are the inconsistencies?

_____

_____

_____

_____

_____

_____

_____

_____

_____

ELITE PERFORMERS

Do more than what is required and are happy to do so. They move independent of coaxing and put in extra time, energy, and effort.

LEVEL PERFORMERS

Do what is minimally required. They show up to work, school, or their kid's music recital but there is no additional investment of time, energy, or effort.

PEAK PERFORMERS

Do what is required and will do more if pushed or asked by someone in authority or by a loved one.

P   E   L

On average, what type of performer have you proven yourself to be up to this point? You can answer based off of your general assessment or from comparing the answers from the data collected above. Has it changed over time,? Does it fluctuate? How you can you maintain?

_____

_____

_____

_____

_____

_____

_____

_____

_____

_____

_____

DAY FOUR: CHANGE IT

What are you going to do to make it from Peak Performance to Elite Performance in your Peak Performing areas?

_____

_____

_____

_____

_____

What are you going to do to move from Level to Peak Performance?

_____

_____

_____

_____

_____

How can moving from one level to the next help you help increase productivity in your career? At home? At school?

_____

_____

_____

_____

_____

Who stands to benefit from you going to the next level?

_____

_____

_____

_____

_____

DAY FIVE: LIVE IT

Question: If a car operates at 6 gears, why would you only drive it on 4? You're wasting potential. Everyone has the potential to be better. Make a move today to move to the next level of performance in two areas of your life (i.e., financially, in your career, in school, etc.). What are you prepared to commit to doing differently that you have not done this year? Create your 7-day plan.

Sunday _____

_____

_____

Monday _____

_____

_____

Tuesday _____

_____

_____

Wednesday _____

_____

_____

Thursday _____

_____

_____

Friday _____

_____

_____

Saturday _____

_____

_____

GREATNESS IS...

Oprah Winfrey is arguably one of the most influential people on the planet. She is one of the best examples of outperforming yourself in the public eye today. Most people know her from her history making talk show, The Oprah Winfrey Show, which was the highest rated program of its time. No one would have blamed her for staying in the pocket and limiting her career to being a phenomenal talk show host, but she didn't stop there. She is CEO of Harpo Productions, CEO of the Oprah Winfrey Network, she founded the Oprah Winfrey Academy for Girls in South Africa, and the list goes on.

If you're already where you want to be in life, that's great, but what's next on the agenda? The potential for success is like a muscle, you have to exercise it if you want to take full advantage of it. If you stop working the muscle, your ability to sustain your status diminishes, and you become a "One Hit Wonder."

Greatness is expanding your portfolio to create more opportunities to stretc.h yourself.

Spend time today reflecting on your actions this week.

Did you meet the challenge? If not, why?

_____

_____

_____

_____

_____

_____

_____

_____

_____

_____

_____

_____

_____

_____

GREATNESS IS UPON YOU

CERTIFICATE OF COMPLETION

This is to certify that

_____

has successfully completed this week's challenge.

Eric Thomas and Associates, LLC

_____
signature

_____
date

PHENOMENAL

GREAT

GOOD

AVERAGE

WEEK 23
KNOCKED DOWN VS. BOUNCE BACK
GREATNESS PRINCIPLE #23:
Greatness is having the fortitude to get up after being knocked down.

When you get hit, are you down for the count or are you back on your feet?

Everyone is capable of success, but most people fail because they aren't able to recover from setbacks. They quit because someone told them that they couldn't do it. They stop because they didn't get the results they expected. They shift gears when it gets too hard.

Indicate which statements apply to you.

☐	I have a history of quitting when things get too hard because I prefer to take an easier route.
☐	When I am faced with disappointments, I'm down for weeks or months at a time before I can get back into a normal routine.
☐	I'm easily distracted from my goals when things don't happen the way that I desire them to.
☐	I allow the goals that I set to be dictated by my failures

Back your answer(s) above with an example from your life:

_____

_____

_____

_____

_____

_____

_____

_____

_____

_____

_____

_____

DAY ONE: LEARN IT

PEOPLE DEAL WITH SETBACKS IN ONE OF THREE WAYS

What setbacks have you encountered in life?

_____

_____

_____

_____

_____

Which category do you fit into?

_____

_____

_____

_____

_____

_____

_____

Sometimes examples help. Everyone falls, but the Greats always manage to land on their feet. Research 3 people that have shown themselves to be examples of resilience. How does your story compare to theirs?

_____

_____

_____

_____

_____

_____

DAY TWO: ACCEPT IT

Complete the following statements:

When dealing with setbacks, I habitually do the following

_____

_____

_____

This usually results in _____

_____

I have (not) been able to meet the following goals due to how I handled the situation

_____

_____

_____

_____

DAY THREE: EMBRACE IT

Create a scenario unique to your life where you are hit with disappointments from multiple directions. Forecast what systems or strategies you would put in place to help you to bounce back on your feet.

_____

_____

_____

_____

_____

DAY FOUR: CHANGE IT

If you have trouble with being resilient, it's never too late in the game to make a change. Many of the lessons we've discussed up to this point are useful in helping you to become more able to adapt to changes in your environment. Visit or revisit the ones that are applicable to your needs:

_____

_____

_____

_____

_____

_____

DAY FIVE: LIVE IT

Don't miss out on anymore opportunities. Create a 7-day plan that will help you to build your resiliency.

Sunday _____

_____

_____

Monday _____

_____

_____

Tuesday _____

_____

Wednesday _____

_____

_____

Thursday _____

_____

_____

Friday _____

_____

_____

Saturday _____

_____

_____

GREATNESS IS...

In 1928, Walt Disney experienced a setback so major that he thought his whole career was on the decline. He made the mistake of signing away the ownership rights to his first successful cartoon to a New York distributor and had to walk away with practically nothing. But this didn't stop him. After getting burned, Walt vowed never to work for anyone else ever again. Walt knew that in order to save his studio, he had to come up with a new character and so was birthed Mickey Mouse and, shortly after, Disneyland.

He learned from his mistake, became knowledgable in intellectual property, continued to work on his craft and now, Walt Disney is a household name. And he was able to accomplish all of this because he never stopped trying.

I told you before, you can't just kind of want it. Sometimes to get back up and keep fighting you have to reach beyond yourself and remember why you set out to do the thing you started to begin with. If you're going to be Great, you've got to have stamina. The race isn't given to the strong, it's given to the ones who can endure.

The problem with many of us, the reason we can't bounce back, is because we lack endurance. We get hit and we stay down, because it's easier to avoid a challenge than it is to stand up to it. We want to compete with the Greats, but we don't even have the courage to get in the ring.

Let me tell you something, an oak tree is just a nut that held it's ground. You don't always have to be smarter, stronger, or faster than the next guy; some fights, you just have to want it enough to stay in the ring.

Greatness is having the fortitude to get up after being knocked down.

Spend time today reflecting on your actions this week.

Did you meet the challenge? If not, why?

_____

_____

_____

_____

_____

_____

_____

_____

_____

_____

_____

_____

_____

_____

_____

_____

_____

_____

GREATNESS IS UPON YOU
CERTIFICATE OF COMPLETION

This is to certify that

_____

has successfully completed this week's challenge.

Eric Thomas and Associates, LLC

_____
signature

_____
date

WEEK 24
WASTED INFORMATION VS. APPLICATION

GREATNESS PRINCIPLE #24:
Greatness is upon you.

Are you wasting information or are you applying it appropriately?

The first step is getting the information. The hard step is applying it. This week we discuss the importance of applying information to your life so that you can begin to see the results you sought the information out for to begin with.

Why do you think that people have a hard time applying information that they've received, even when its good?

_____

_____

_____

_____

_____

_____

_____

_____

_____

_____

_____

_____

_____

_____

_____

_____

DAY ONE: LEARN IT

How many opportunities have you missed out on because you failed to apply your knowledge on the subject?

_____

_____

_____

_____

_____

_____

_____

_____

DAY TWO: ACCEPT IT

Consider the chapters in this book that were most applicable to your life. In the space below, indicate what lessons you learned; in the space next to it, note whether you have successfully applied those lessons to your life.

_____

_____

_____

_____

_____

_____

_____

_____

_____

DAY THREE: EMBRACE IT

Getting the information is only

STEP 1

STEP 2-100

... involves applying it!

EXTRA STEPS

What extra steps can you take today to add the necessary pressure you need to realize your full potential?

What extra steps can you take today to add the necessary pressure you need to realize your full potential? For example, maybe you need to recommit yourself to your purpose, or maybe you need to spend extra time in a few of the chapters in this book until the lessons become second nature.

DAY FOUR: CHANGE IT

Change can begin as early as today. Before diving head first into a project or opportunity, stop and ask yourself...

Do I have the information I need to get started?

_____

_____

_____

Do I know the correct way in which to apply the information?

_____

_____

_____

Am I willing to deal with the pressure associated with the task?

_____

_____

_____

What can I do to push myself to be consistent and demand change?

_____

_____

_____

_____

What lessons or information from this book can you share with someone you know?

_____

_____

_____

_____

_____

_____

DAY FIVE: LIVE IT
Now that you have the information, what plan will you put in gear to apply the information to your own life?

Sunday _____

_____

Monday _____

_____

Tuesday _____

_____

Wednesday _____

_____

Thursday _____

_____

Friday _____

_____

_____

Saturday _____

_____

_____

GREATNESS IS...

You can be Great.

I started studying the Greats, and what I realize about the Greats is that it's not about talent. The difference between the Good and the Great is about Mentality - it's all or nothing. What you did last week doesn't count, you are as current as the present moment, you have to play every single play as if it were your last. And you have to play it with the mindset of a Champion - "I can. I Will. I MUST."

The Greats didn't necessarily wake up every morning thinking, "Today, I'm going to be Great." But the thing that separates them from everyone else is that they got up every day and did the ordinary extraordinarily.

Greatness isn't something that happens over night. It's an ongoing process that starts with waking up everyday and taking full advantage of the time and opportunities that have been gifted to you.

I get out of bed every morning at 3 am, and I pour 120% into every opportunity that God has given me. Because when I go out to speak, my son is depending on me, my daughter is depending on me... my wife and mom are depending on me... my company depends on me. There are children all over the country who watch me and say, "... if ET can be a high school dropout and take 12 years to get a 4-year degree and now be only weeks away from getting his PhD, then I've got a chance..."

I don't get to let them down. My excuses won't provide them with what they need. I've got an opportunity of a lifetime, and I've got to take advantage of it.

When we began, I told you that this book was an opportunity for you to rewrite your history. It doesn't matter if you've failed to meet your goals. It doesn't matter that you've endured disappointment after disappointment. It doesn't matter that you're not where life says you should be at this stage in your life. And it doesn't matter how selfish, self-centered, or self-involved you were in your past, or how many opportunities you've missed or waited too long for. All that matters is the answer to this question today: Now that you have information that could change your life, what are you going to do about it? Are you going to take advantage of it? Or will you let it sit and collect dust?

Greatness is upon you.

Spend time today reflecting on your actions this week.

Did you meet the challenge? If not, why?

GIUY RE-UP

AVERAGE PEOPLE	GREATNESS...
Get permanently distracted by disappointments.	*Requires perseverance.*
Are prone to only trust what they can see.	*Requires vision.*
Replay the same success story.	*Requires making yourself your biggest competition and then outperforming yourself.*
Frequently lack elasticity.	*Requires an ability to bounce back.*
Obtain information and rarely apply it.	

Assess how well you've demonstrated your potential in this area on the scales below:

Before Reading :

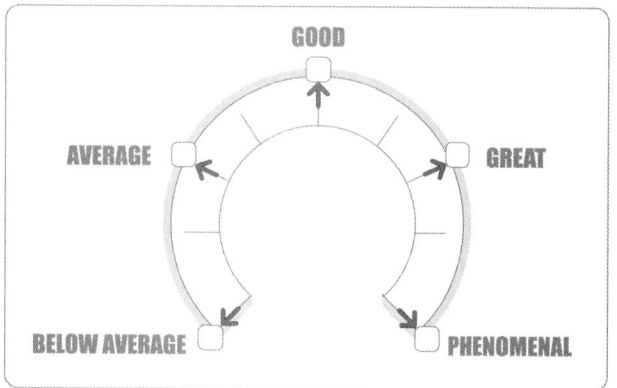

After Reading :

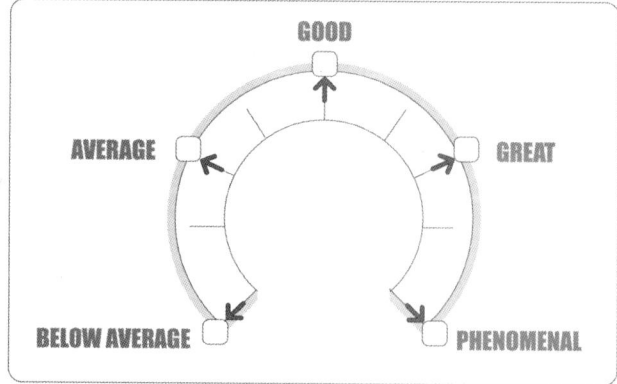

GREATNESS IS UPON YOU

CERTIFICATE OF COMPLETION

This is to certify that

_____

has successfully completed this week's challenge.

Eric Thomas and Associates, LLC

_____
signature

_____
date

GREATNESS IS UPON YOU
ACCOUNTABILITY AGREEMENT

This is to certify that I,

_____

have agreed to be

_____ 's

accountability partner.

I am committed to being a support system and
partner in the growth and development of

_____

in her/his professional life.

Eric Thomas and Associates, LLC

_____
signature

_____
date

GREATNESS IS UPON YOU
ACCOUNTABILITY AGREEMENT

This is to certify that I,

_____

have agreed to be

_____'s

accountability partner.

I am committed to being a support system and partner in the growth and development of

_____

in her/his professional life.

Eric Thomas and Associates, LLC

_____
signature

_____
date

Welcome to
Breathe University™

A holistic approach to success, involving a series of one on one intimate instructional sessions with Inspirational Speaker and Life Strategist, Eric Thomas, to help you transform your life in the areas of: Finances, Relationships, Career Goals, Marriage and more!

For more information contact:
info@BreatheUniversity.com or call 866-526-3978

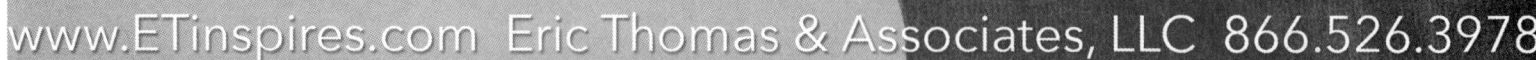